A Twilight of Owls

Jessie and Leon
With kind regards
Jennit, Xmas 98

A TWILIGHT OF OWLS

JENNIE GRAY

THE GARGOYLE'S HEAD

The Gargoyle's Head Press Ltd
Chatham House, Gosshill Road
Chislehurst, Kent BR7 5NS

Printed in Great Britain by Antony Rowe Ltd
ISBN 1-874100 12 8

For Mum and Ken

When cats run home and night is come,
And dew is cold upon the ground,
And the far-off stream is dumb,
And the whirring sail goes round,
And the whirring sail goes round,
Alone and warming his five wits,
The white owl in the belfry sits.

Tennyson

I have sent unto you ... a beast, the creature of God, sometime wild, but now tame, to comfort your heart at such time as you be weary of praying.

A monk of Christ Church, Canterbury, to Lady Lisle 1536

Gilbert White, Selborne, July 8, 1773

We have had, ever since I can remember, a pair of white owls that constantly breed under the eaves of this church. As I have paid good attention to the manner of life of these birds during their season of breeding, which lasts the summer through, the following remarks may not perhaps be unacceptable: About an hour before sunset (for then the mice begin to run) they sally forth in quest of prey, and hunt all round the hedges of meadows and small enclosures for them, which seem to be their only food. In this irregular country we can stand on an eminence and see them beat the fields over like a setting-dog, and often drop down in the grass or corn. I have minuted these birds, with my watch for an hour together, and have found that they return to their nests, the one or the other of them, about once in five minutes; reflecting at the same time on the adroitness that every animal is possessed of as regards the well-being of itself and offspring. But a piece of address, which they show when they return loaded, should not, I think, be passed over in silence. — As they take their prey with their claws, so they carry it in their claws to their nest: but, as the feet are necessary in their ascent under the tiles, they constantly perch first on the roof of the chancel, and shift the mouse from their claws to their bill, that the feet may be at liberty to take hold of the plate on the wall as they are rising under the eaves.

White owls seem not (but in this I am not positive) to hoot at all: all that clamorous hooting appears to me to come from the wood kinds. The white owl does indeed snore and hiss in a tremendous manner; and these menaces will answer the intention of intimidating: for I have known a whole village up in arms on such an occasion, imagining the church-yard to be full of goblins and spectres. White owls also often scream horribly as they fly along; from this screaming probably arose the common people's imaginary species of screech-owl, which they superstitiously think attends the windows of dying persons. The plumage of the remiges of the wings of every species of owl that I have yet examined is remarkably soft and pliant. Perhaps it may be necessary that the wings of these birds should not make much resistance or rushing, that they may be enabled to steal through the air unheard upon a nimble and watchful quarry.

While I am talking of owls, it may not be improper to mention what I was told by a gentleman of the county of Wilts. As they were grubbing a vast hollow pollard-ash that had been the mansion of owls for centuries, he discovered at the bottom a mass of matter that at first he could not account for. After some examination, he found it was a congeries of the bones of mice (and perhaps of birds and bats) that had been heaping together for ages, being cast up in pellets out of the crops of many generations of inhabitants. For owls cast up the bones, fur and feathers of what they devour, after the manner of hawks. He believes, he told me, that there were bushels of this kind of substance.

Chapter One - Decisions

10th April 1995

Stefan had been sitting around all morning in the spring sunshine. He had 'manned' the steppes eagle, the harris hawk, and the nervous junior peregrine, but at some stage he had also gone to check on the barn owls and had discovered that the first of the eggs had hatched.

When Alan and I got back, Stefan had the pleasure of telling us the news and remarking that Alan never knew what was happening in his own garden. We all went up to have a look. It was dark in the aviary even though the roof was mostly wire mesh. There were some unkempt elderberry trees, nettles, coarse grass and weeds, which cut down the interior space and made it seem smaller and more cramped than it really was. The whole den was forlorn, and rank, and rather smelly. In the filthy dust bath in the corner lay the four remaining small white eggs. She was huddled next to them, hours old and not a pretty sight, a helpless minuscule purplish bag of flesh with top-heavy head and blind crusted eyes.

Behind us, on a high platform, her parents glowered down at us. They had already attacked us once, swooping down soundlessly, one, then the other — then one of them had wheeled back and raked me across the knee. I was rather enchanted by this, the first time I had ever been attacked by an owl. I was in the honeymoon period, when everything is enthralling, and cuts, gashes, bruises, and multiple lacerations all seem part of the delicious fun. The lightness, the thistledown lightness of the birds was unbelievable — it was like being mugged by a miniature rosebush.

'We better go now, the parents will be getting too upset.'

We edged out sideways, and Alan, who had broken the

padlock off because he had lost the key, rolled a big rock against the door to keep it shut.

Later in the afternoon, Alan and I took the trained barn owl out into the next door field. Imaginatively called Owly, he is very very pale, ghostly white underneath like a moonbeam. He spent most of the time running after Alan with hilarious little splayed flatfooted movements — he seems to find flying a bit of a fag altogether. Once or twice Alan picked him up on the glove and gently threw him in the direction of a tree, but he still lacked the incentive to go up and just drifted gently down again towards ground level. I couldn't keep my eyes off his silvered dainty prettiness, and at last he condescended to float up into a tree with all the stress and effort of a helium balloon.

Naturally when we got back and Alan said about finding homes for the owlets, I said I would have one. I wanted the one hatched that day, the one which I had seen. That was fine with Alan. I kept wondering if it worked the same way as with puppies, where the first-born is usually the pick of the litter. But Alan said nothing about this possibility, and I cunningly kept quiet in case my theory was pure rubbish.

20th April

I did not see my tiny owlet again till yesterday, and then it was only for the briefest glimpse through the small food-door which lets down in the plywood wall. She was two or three times as large, but just as puny and ugly as ever. There was a sibling with her, half or a third her size. It is the last of the brood — one of the remaining eggs was accidentally smashed, and the other two proved to be infertile.

We took Owly over the fields again. It's lambing time and there have been a few casualties. Alan said the carcases were not taken away by the Ministry of Agriculture any more, so the farmers had to dispose of them themselves. A funeral pyre, which we had seen in the process of being built last week, had been set alight but had burned poorly and gone out. The foxes had removed various pieces of roast mutton from the fire, and had scattered them here and there over the field. There was a charred leg, and a haunch, and a blackened skull with all its teeth showing. Bits of greyish dirty-looking wool, in long strands and hanks, lay about everywhere, as if someone had been tearing apart a collection of barristers' wigs.

Further on a ewe had just given birth, and her lamb, wet and sticky, staggered to its feet as we approached and followed its mother, who was hurrying away. The afterbirth lay flaccid and red across the grass, an elongated membrane like a popped balloon. Alan warned me to get the owl away from it, as if he saw it he would fly down and gorge himself. To bribe the owl to keep following me (for he would only come to the glove for food), I had to keep tearing little ragged bits off the day-old chick in my bag. The chicks are the by-products of the egg industry, the males, which are culled at one day old because they have no commercial value. What you get is a tiny floppy enervated little body, covered in Disney-yellow fur, with clean pink feet and tiny stubby wings. The stomach contains the remains of the egg yolk, which bursts out at the most inconvenient moments. The chick doesn't seem to have a single bone in its body — in fact the whole thing is runny and liquefied in the extreme. My fingers were soon covered with blood and sticky sludge. There was no way of washing this accumulating mess off, and as usual I ended up feeling totally disgusted by what I was doing.

So why indulge in such a revolting activity? The answer has to be that it is just amazing to be so close to such beautiful creatures, birds which I have either never seen before or have only glimpsed in the most fleeting fashion. Their miraculous acceptance of human beings and their lack of fear of them are a complete revelation. Their beauty is astounding, astonishing, miraculous. Their alien nature is just as intriguing, their complete Martian strangeness — they are a world totally apart from the mammals to which we belong — there is something almost reptilian about them — cold-blooded, lizard-like. At least that's what I thought when I first met the Harris hawks at Gleneagles — now I'm not so sure.

It was last September, and I was on a two-day falconry course. The first day was just a training day at the Centre, but the second day we drove up into the hills with two Harris hawks. Harrises are the only hawks who will hunt cooperatively, as a team, not turn on one another and rip each other to shreds. D.J. the male, was a bright-eyed inquisitive irresistible little enthusiast. Scotland the female, was considerably larger and more powerful — something like a small eagle to my inexperienced eyes. She looked magnificent and very imperious gliding from tree to tree, always settling on the strong lower branches whilst D.J chose the thin high branches above her (and even then, she would sometimes knock him off out of pure prima donna arrogance). Both of them wore little brass bells, which jingled melodiously whenever they moved, melancholy, charming, a most romantic music. The bells are to guide the falconer if the birds are lost from sight, but the drawback is that the quarry soon come to know the sound, and go to ground or hide in thick cover the minute that they hear it. On this particular morning they all absented themselves immediately. We walked for a long time in the woods and caught nothing.

I was not in the least bit sorry. It had only occurred to me that morning that was what falconry was about — Killing

Things.

Now I realised the implications, they were so blindingly obvious, so in-your-face, that it had taken a certain kind of cretinous genius to miss them. My excuse was that before that outing I hadn't really given the matter any considered thought. What falconry had meant to me was the Middle Ages — my ideas were based on medieval tapestries, relics of a long-lost dreamworld in which the dyes had faded so much over the centuries that all the violent red had been leached out. Blue-green was the dominating colour. There were forests and meadows bedecked with flowers, wan pale-faced lords and ladies, and horses, dogs, hawks and quarry frozen in strange but graceful postures. These images did not seem to show blood sports at all, but rather a series of endless afternoon picnics with delightful animal and bird companions.

When I arrived at Gleneagles, I was still under the thrall of this charming Pre-Fall illusion. Everything about the hotel seemed to back it up — the tapestries in the bar had the same type of hunting scene, albeit four centuries later, a wispy couple on horseback meandering through a wood exchanging amorous confidences. In our suite there were two pictures of hawking scenes, in one of which a Victorian couple, the lady dressed immaculately in long riding habit, hat and floating veil, posed outside the gates of their park. There was a menial wandering round in the background wearing what appeared to be a bizarre sort of wooden petticoat — it was a cadge, dependent by straps from his shoulders, an apparatus of bars on which sat various hooded falcons. In the foreground of the picture there was a scene which should have struck some kind of warning note, but did not. Another liveried menial, beautifully dressed, was bending over a recumbent heron, and that heron appeared to be sicking up its breakfast — eels, fish, frogs, small fresh-water crustaceans, etcetera, in a tidal wave from its long beak. The title of the picture was 'Disgorging'. I hadn't got a clue what was going on in this peculiar picture, but all the humans looked insufferably smug whilst the heron gave no indication at all of enjoying itself.

I did not heed the warning of the picture. There were too many other distractions on that first day. It was a beautiful September afternoon, so warm that it was delightful to lie on the close-clipped lawn, and watch the pretty grey wagtails, of which there were scores, dipping and running about the grass. Eventually I even got round to asking the doorman whether there were still any eagles in the vicinity. He had obviously been asked this inane question a million times. He said no, there were never any eagles this far south; it was a corruption of some french word which meant 'church' — Gleneagles meant 'Glen of the Church'.

It didn't take a great linguist to work out the missing french word was 'église'. I also noticed that the hotel wasn't going to pass up the opportunity of having carved stone eagles everywhere around the place.

It was only when we got out of the jeep with the Harris hawks two days later, on an extremely unattractive, bald and brutalised Scottish hillside, that my beautiful ideal suddenly died, its ghost drifting away in a puff of smoke. The truth about falconry became crystal clear in an instant. I felt embarrassed by my crass stupidity, yet also obscurely thwarted and cheated.

And then there were the practical problems to deal with. I have never been a hunter, never liked the chase, always felt an intense visceral disgust at the idea of killing other living creatures for fun. I had to announce my moral qualms to the guy I had come out with, who took it remarkably well under the circumstances, merely remarking teasingly after he had got over the immediate shock: 'Well, we'll just have to have a lot of pretty flying about then'.

In the event, at the very end of the day, we actually did catch one rabbit. I didn't even see the doomed creature before D.J. had it. He leaped off the glove before I could stop him, his jesses slipping through the wet leather with the force of his taking off. It was all over in an instant — no scream, no blood, no spectacle, no drama — except that Scotland went down a split second afterwards and knocked poor D.J. off his catch. It must have been like being hit by a feathered tidal wave. One minute he was on the rabbit, the next minute he was off it and lying in the grass on his back. The shock was as nothing to his hurt feelings. He lay there, with his yellow talons stuck preposterously in the air, screaming insult after raucous insult at her.

She took absolutely no notice of him. Now she crouched over the fallen prey, completely covering it by spreading out her wings and her tail until from above she looked exactly like a huge circular fan. This mantling was to protect her catch from notice, from anyone who might wish to steal that rabbit from her just as she had stolen it from D.J. She appeared to the casual eye quite still and motionless, but beneath the circular cover of her wings she was gluttonously pecking and tearing away. It seemed poor little D.J. wasn't even going to get a look in. But then he caught sight of one tip of the rabbit's foot, just sticking out beneath her tail, and seeing no reason why she should have it all, launched himself on it and began to chew it.

He was mantling too and you couldn't see that rabbit for wings. They were like mesmerised spirits, caught in a dream, in a web that was millions of years old, possessed wholly by that spell of instinct, that age-old impulse to gorge and bloat. How passionately they adored that rabbit, how hot was the love they felt for it, and how closely they hung over it, covering and protecting it with their wings, pecking and tearing at its still warm flesh. They would have stayed there feeding till they could hardly move for gluttony, had not James eventually bribed them off.

When I got back to the hotel Jon asked me 'What was it like?'

And I replied 'Weird'.

The birds had seemed to me like creatures from another planet. They were absolutely nothing like mammals at all. They were reptilian, primaeval, an alien species with whom a human being had very little in common — to be with them was to peer through a glass darkly into a world of almost incomprehensible strangeness. I had been intrigued and repelled in equal measure.

We were at the hotel for five more days, but I did not go back to do another day's falconry. I thought about it in a half-hearted way, but being in a completely ambiguous state of mind finally decided to give it a miss.

But I couldn't forget the sight of the birds flying free and yet returning willingly to a human being's call. So that's why, six months later, I'm on the course at Alan's.

Alan's most striking bird is Alaska, the Bald Eagle — immensely imperious and arrogant-looking, with her hooked yellow beak and savage-browed eyes. She is still in her juvenile plumage, and will not get the adult's magnificent white head and neck until she is three years old. When he takes her flying, the pair of them look very good together, because he has just the right touch of raffish frontiersman about him, with his tall lean build and the scar running from his mouth into his cheek. She is his favourite of all the birds. He also has the lanner falcon, two peregrines, a kestrel, a steppes eagle, a goshawk, a harris hawk, a european eagle owl, the barn owls, and sundry disabled wild birds, including tawny owls, in the aviaries at the back.

Alaska is hugely impressive but I don't much care for her. It is the kestrel and the nearly all-white barn owl who attract me, the tiny birds, their accessibility, their perfect fragile beauty. How can anything so small and so daintily built live entirely by catching and killing? Owly is a bit of a scruff on closer acquaintance, with broken tatty feathers and bald patches under his wing, though he is still extremely pretty when floating airily at a distance. The kestrel, a female, is exquisite, painted with the sharpness and clarity of a Hilliard miniature. She is a nervous little creature, nothing like as laid back and placid as him, and when I walk up to her she tries to escape, flying away to the full length of her jesses and leash which bring her up with a start and jolt her back to the ground. If I pick her up, she gives a high sobbing cry, both infinitely mournful and full of indignation.

Everything about these wondrous birds is very new and very strange to me. Alan kept pointing to his band where they were tethered on their perches on the lawn — 'Look, they've seen something up there'. I would look and see the birds, from the eagles to the falcons to the hawks, staring upwards into the sky. It was good weather most of the time, a bright azure heaven with huge white clouds, and it was by these clouds that you would pinpoint the birds of prey flying impossibly high overhead — mere pinprick dots, or a winged form only just distinguishable as such — 'See that big cloud there, the one with ragged edge, it's roughly about the centre of that now' — then I would locate some minuscule black atom.

I never realised before how high the birds fly. The second day I was at Alan's we went out with the lanner falcon, and finding a thermal it soared up and up and up until it was no bigger than the dot at the end of this sentence. The sky was so bright that as I went on staring up at it, tears began to run down my face even though I was wearing sunglasses. There were four of us watching the lanner — me, Jon, Alan and Stefan (who said in a pitying, amiably contemptuous sort of way 'you *have* got bad eyesight, haven't you?') — and every so often we would all lose sight of the lanner and then someone would find it again, give directions, bearings, using the shape of the clouds, and we would all see it again. Then it truly disappeared — no one could find it — you realised the stupendous vastness of the blue space you were staring into and how you would never be able to find that minuscule black dot in it. All that was left was the regular blip of the transmitter, for the bird wore a minute tracking device on its tail.

Fifteen anxious minutes went past. It seemed all too likely that the bird had gone forever. Then quite suddenly, unexpectedly, the signal grew stronger, and all at once the lanner appeared, not plummeting out of the heavens as I had expected but coming with inches to spare over the tall trees at the end of the field and immediately right down to the ground, shooting across the grass at immense speed only six or eight inches up, its little pointed evil face and dark eyes shining, until suddenly it swooped up again and struck the lure with massive force.

I was highly impressed with the lanner, but I do not covet it. What I want is the calm serene amiability of Owly, and I have soppy fantasies about my own tame barn owl floating through a summer twilight, or through the gauzy mist rising off a water meadow, or flying silently down to perch on a mossy gravestone whose ancient inscription is half-obscured. A lot of romantic twaddle in other words.

15th May

We go to Alan's to pick up the owlet. She is 35 days old, and has been hand-reared since 22 days old, with her small brother or sister joining her in the house a few days later.

I have no idea whether 'she' really is a she or not. It's a complicated task sexing birds, and most people just guess at this stage and find out the truth later. I have decided she is a she because that is what I want, and because she hatched first, and the female is the favoured sex in the world of birds of prey.

With an assumed sex had come an assumed name. I'm calling her 'Hesper', the evening star. Well, Hesper, cost me £35 with 10 days supply of food and everything else cost me about £1,800. There was a surprising number of pieces of equipment to purchase. Have had two immense aviaries put up in the garden, and a cheaper small one for Buddy, the flightless crow.

There's been a last minute panic to get everything in place for Hesper's arrival. Everything must be prepared and waiting — this is what is sternly counselled by the experts in the books I keep nervously reading and re-reading. I have obediently assembled the dusting powder, the vitamin supplements, the weighing machine, and all the rest of the paraphernalia. I spent hours searching the local shops for a meatgrinder to mince her food, and only finally located one in an old-fashioned ironmonger's on the way to collect her. The aviary which she won't be able to use for weeks, because she is too little to be outside by herself, has been aesthetically kitted out with a dead tree and several immense rolls of wood, purloined from across the stream where the estate people sawed up the willow that fell on our garden. The floor material of the aviary is the finest white sand and each bag as I poured it out weighed about as much as a planet and daintily covered less area than a pocket handkerchief. More bags are therefore on order.

I'm all excited when I go to Alan's — I'm really excited about Hesper. I'm not sure how big she'll be, how grown-up looking — I'm excited and nervous at the same time.

What I actually see when we get there is the minutest scrap of very grubby off-white fuzz with a distinctly off-putting pong to it. Put bluntly, she's hideous — she looks like a million year old witch with a hangover, with her sharp pointed pale nose and immense purple rings round her black eyes. She's friendly and cute though, making the prettiest most un-owl-like cheeping noise, whilst next to her her sibling (who has caught up with her in size) hisses in threat and bombastic fury at us strangers.

Looking at the true-life Hesper I'm appalled. Romantic visions fly out of the window when faced with the reality of a five week old owlet. She attempts to stand, but she's totally unsteady on her feet, she wavers and pulsates, then plops back on her bottom. This owl surely has months to go before she can walk, let alone fly. She has no muscular control whatsoever. Nor does she give the slightest promise of beauty, in fact completely and utterly the reverse. She has bleary little black eyes with scabby crusted lashes, and two chicken wings folded in the strangest way — they have three planes in them, not two, as in my ignorance of birds I had always assumed. As a finishing touch, despite the grubby fluff, bits of witch-like skin show everywhere and she looks naked.

Feeling morose and gloomy, I go outside to search for Owly, to reassure myself that the hideous little monstrosity in the trailer is going to turn into something delectable like him. Alan's got a second trained owl now, the brother of Hesper from a brood two years previously. I saw him in the aviary the morning Hesper hatched, and Alan's last action on leaving was to catch him as he flew past, his long white legs trailing, and remove him from the home which he shared with his parents. Alan let him stay with them last year, and another brood hatched, and then suddenly all the little owlets were found dead, murdered probably by their year-old brother. Barn owls are supposed to be tolerant and peaceable towards one another as a general rule —they are not violently territorial like tawnies for example — but fratricide is sometimes committed by older siblings and the finger definitely points at this one.

Despite his Ivan the Terrible reputation, he is a dainty, pretty, fragile-looking little thing. We are strangers and he doesn't like us, so he puts on the full barn-owl threat display — wings held tautly out so as to make him appear larger than he really is, head moving slowly from side to side, a piercing angry hiss emanating from his beak. His movements are so stylised, so deliberate and mechanical, so carefully choreographed and done so exactly to a pattern, that he doesn't appear to be a living creature at all but rather some gorgeous little clockwork toy.

We go back to the changelings in the trailer. Alan examines my brand-new mincer, and nearly has a fit when I say how much it had cost me (£19.95). 'I could have sold you one for that' he says, rummaging amongst the ironmongery in the corner and producing a spidery, grey, gangling, antique object which looks about as hygienic as a septic tank. My up-to-the-hour model comes dismantled, and he and Jon get quite interested in the problems of assembling it, putting together the various disparate parts. Once it is in working order, Alan puts in a white mouse and starts cranking. 'It's not working. It can't be strong enough.' But eventually the little corpse goes slowly down into the innards and is spewed out the other end in the most excruciating mess of oozing, bloody-red and white chunks and globules. I wonder for the millionth time exactly why I'm doing this.

Since Hesper's been hand-reared by them, things have changed. Alan's wife, Sally, has taken a fancy to her, and it is Alan's job to persuade me to take the second owlet. 'Now don't let this influence you, you can have whichever one you want, but Sally's got rather fond of that one.' To aid his powers of persuasion, he takes out the second owlet, the one that hisses, puts it on a board on the table and turns it this way and that to show it off. The problem is that sis/bro is even more unutterably hideous (if that were possible) than Hesper, and moreover comes utterly unendowed with the charm of having been thought about and dreamed about for five weeks. Sis/bro has no chance. But I like Sally very much, and I don't know what to do about the impasse. Meanwhile the hideous one continues with its cross mood and hisses furiously at me. Know I must have the putative Hesper or feel diddled for all eternity. Alan continues showing off the scrawny evil bag, whilst so-called Hesper reposes sweetly and if awakened at any time only utters the most delicious melodious chittering. Grit teeth and resolve *not* to be self-sacrificing. 'Well, I don't want to cause Sally any grief, but I really do prefer the non-hissy one.' 'Settled then,' says Alan, who has done his duty as a husband — he returns the hideous one to the basket, and we all start talking and laughing about something else.

Five minutes later Sally turns up, in a big breathless rush, as if she has dashed back from somewhere for an eleventh hour rescue operation. Their son comes in too, all sulky and cross, goes up to his father and whispers very audibly 'She [meaning me] can't have *that* one.' He then demands if he can ride his bike and vanishes. Veiled but extremely amiable tussle of will commences. Somehow the positions are reversed and I offer twice to give up my pet and Sally resolutely tells me that no, I must have it if that is the one I want. It *is* the one I want, and at half past four Jon and I depart with Hesper. I feel a vague sense of callousness and guilt, but Alan says that the children don't want either of the owlets to go, and that they will just ask to keep them both and then do nothing with them, just get bored with them and spend their time doing other things — So THAT'S ALL RIGHT THEN.

Hesper travels back from Alan's beautifully, she makes no fuss. Nor, when we get home, does she object to the parrot cage in which we have decided to keep her until she gets bigger, the bars acting as protection from the cats and dogs, not as an imprisonment to keep her in. She has some soft rags to sleep on and she flops down and goes to sleep at once. Shortly Rowley, a sleek handsome black cat with a white collar like a vicar, strolls in for a bite of supper. He gets up on his chair and, looking across to the counter, become aware of the monstrous filthy white bundle in the cage. He does a double-take, aghast and appalled. Horror couldn't be more vividly painted than in those round gold staring eyes, blazing like headlamps.

Later the dogs are introduced through the bars of the cage and get in a big state about the newcomer. Sasha in particular seems to think it's a puppy when it makes its high chittering cry.

I'm exhausted, and I drink too much whisky as an aid to recovery, which doesn't work, and find myself to my great amazement drunk in the kitchen at half past ten at night, preparing a gore-fest for our new acquisition. I have rats, mice and chicks, and they are all equally dead and equally repellent. Shutting my eyes to what I'm doing, I hack off bits of rat for a sacrificial offering. A querulous voice at the back of my skull enquires how the hell I've got mixed up in this. I can't believe what I'm doing, I must be insane. I fight back a well-nigh irresistible impulse to puke. Once cut up, the bloody titbits can be fed to Hesper, with some teensy show of hygiene, with a pair of tweezers. I say to Jon 'Will you feed her before you go to bed?' Jon says very pleasantly 'Yes'. He's always liked little baby things more than me — he's practically going itchy-gitchy-goo over Hesper. Me, I can't wait for her to grow up so she can chop up her own disgusting supper.

Chapter Two - Bringing up Baby

16th May

Owlet does nothing all day but sleep, shit, and eat dismembered bits of rats and mice.

Around seven o'clock in the evening she commences some stretching exercises. She stand up as best as she can and proceeds to put her wings up and out over her neck. She looks like a person in a straitjacket trying to get out of it once the sleeves have been untied. The fluff she is wearing even has the same colour, a sort of nasty medical off-white.

A few minutes later something really upsets her. She goes into full threat display, clopping her beak, hissing, really upset, staring fixedly out through the window in the back door. It takes us a while to work out what has frightened her, but finally we decide it must be the tall trees outside thrashing about in a summer gale. They must look like great green giants advancing, flailing their immense arms, tossing their dreadlocked heads. Hesper warns them loudly to BACK OFF. Jon says 'You won't scare them away like that, you know'. She goes on hissing, louder and louder. At last, to calm her down, I carry the cage into the sitting room. The cat flees in horror at the hissing cacophony.

Hesper calms down almost immediately. She teeters about the cage like a drunk and then stops still and inspects her feet. Jon says she has been staring at her feet all day admiringly, as if to say haven't I got beautiful feet.

Jon is still very keen on the new baby and hangs over the cage for hours stuffing bits of food down it (all of which, on butcher's duty, *I* have cut up). Hesper swallows several enormous lumps, and then plays lackadaisically with a chick leg for half an hour — first it is in, then it is out, finally she drops it in her bed, at which point I seize it primly and throw it away.

The bedding gets dirty really quickly and has to be washed every day. It's hard to imagine how bad a real barn owl nest must smell, with a hen bird and four or five chicks constantly crapping and regurgitating pellets everywhere. The hens get so filthy and bedraggled that the first thing they do when they can leave the young is go and find somewhere to have a bath. Sometimes they are drowned in cattle drinking troughs, into which they have hurled themselves in a fervour of impatience to get clean. Their feathers become waterlogged, they cannot get out, and then a pathetic little corpse floats in the death-bath.

Jon is very amused by the owl but insists on calling her Nelly.

'Don't call her Nelly — it will stick.'

But the next time I see her I call her 'Smelly Nelly'.

'Hesper' does seem absurdly high-flown for this undignified, grubby ball of fluff.

19th May

The owlet's pet name has become Hespernelli, pronounced Sicilian Godfather style, with an exaggerated flourish on the last two syllables.

She remains as chronically ugly as ever. Black button eyes with a bluish sheen to them like a drunk's, like the drunk she resembles as she staggers about looking as if she is going to topple over. Round her eyes are immense bald purplish patches of skin. Her head looks skeletal, with its narrow skull-like shape and pale hooked nose. Round her beak there is a vile collection of rusty-stained whiskers, daubed with the remains of blood and food. She has the most absurd stub of a tail. Her fluff is sort of debauched ostrich, soft, substanceless, airy and delicate, which might be charming if it were pure white but which instead has a seedy, dirty, septic, hospital laundry look.

Lovely are the curves of the white owl sweeping
Wavy in the dusk lit by one large star. *George Meredith.*

Well, we're a long way from that kind of beauty yet.

It is quite obvious that the feathers are growing rapidly beneath the fluff, because when she stretches her wing out you can see the quills, the flight feathers, the critical primary feathers without which she would never be able to fly, emerging beneath like a skeletal fan. If you ruffle back the fluff on her back or stomach, you see great bald patches of skin underneath, but here and there instead there is a really dense patchwork or network of quills. They don't seem to lie in a pattern (though no doubt they do, I'm just missing the logic of it) but crisscross madly all over the place. As the new feathers begin to emerge, it must itch frantically — I imagine Hespernelli must be feeling one enormous itch all over.

I only noticed yesterday — or was it the day before? — the perfect star shape she makes with her claws when she stands properly — they are not Y or H but X — and they look very pretty when she manages that. She has all of a sudden, very quickly, mastered the art of standing — before that, most of the time lying down, she had little cramped-up, bunched-up, arthritic-looking feet. No wonder she likes contemplating her new arrangement. The muscular tremor has almost completely vanished. The last two days have seen a major transformation in her — she seems twice the size she was on Monday, though this may partly be because she is standing as opposed to squatting. Her shape seems to have changed too — she is more owl-like, less of Frankenstein's baby. Is it an illusion or has that fantastic grotesque ugliness been ameliorated one jot? I don't think it is an illusion — she is almost certainly looking better. I don't think this is some quasi-maternal prejudice — I've never been able to lean over this particular cradle and coo 'How sweet!'

Other people's reactions to the owl have been very instructive: Brenda adored it; Julie, Paddy and Graham were bemused but quite taken with it; Gary and his girlfriend were frankly disgusted. No one is indifferent or uninterested.

There's a new system of housekeeping which is working quite well. I make a nest of rags in one corner of the cage, and cover the rest of the floor with newspaper. Hesper just about manages to score on the newspaper when she mutes, though the boundaries are often pretty fuzzy.

When she's been out and about, she creeps chittering into the hole I've created in the middle of the rag pile, flops down and goes to sleep. She is very conscientious about at least *trying* to shit outside the nest, but she dumps her pellets in her bed with gay abandon. In one of my books it says that pellets are the only nesting material that barn owls use, and that in old established nests there is a thick warm pile of them. Perhaps this is why Hesper insists on dumping pellets in her bed. They are not offensive, even though Sally described them as 'big, black and wet, looking like a dog turd'. They don't smell, and are only damp on the surface rather than wet through, so they soon dry out. They are compact and hard. Mostly they consist of fur, mixed up with little bits of crushed bone, all looking minced but otherwise not much altered for having passed through Hesper's digestive system. Barn owls have a low acidity in their stomachs, which is generally estimated at about the strength of vinegar.

In old nests, the pellets attract clothes moths, which eat

the fur, then pupate in the pellet, and emerge as adult moths. At some point in the past centuries they must have migrated from the owl pellet to the human wardrobe — an interesting theory, which I can't be bothered to explore right now.

In damp nest sites, the owl pellets grow mould. This leads onto another strange old story, about ghost owls who used to glow in the dark and terrify the country folk as they swept soundlessly through the churchyard on luminous wings. The Hound of the Baskerville look was due to phosphorescent bacteria or honey fungus. The owls had been roosting in hollow trees, and particles of the bacteria had dusted the birds' plumage and given them their strange spectral appearance.

Hesper continues to stuff the most amazing quantities of food away. I've made progress with my butchery, and though I am not inured to it, I don't feel quite so much like puking when I take a pair of kitchen scissors to a tiny mouse or chick. I have never used the state-of-the-art mincing machine, because the thought of cleaning it out afterwards is too unutterably repellent. Instead I wield a sharp pair of kitchen scissors. One thing I always do is to snip the chicks' stomachs and let the yolk go down the sink — I hate that mess sticking everywhere. Then I snip off the bird's head, its little dangling legs — it's horror movie stuff — I feel like Quentin Tarantino let loose in the Walt Disney archives.

But then we've all got so ridiculously far from the truth of what we eat — the beef, lamb, pork, mutton, turkey, which always comes wrapped in nice hygienic packages, covered in cellophane and pretty labels. These sanitised lumps bear no relation at all to the animals which lost their lives, or the manner in which they were carved up, their innards spilled out, their heads cut off, their feet, hooves, fur or feathers removed. Acting as Hesper's butcher every day I keep seeing that process very graphically, and in a way it makes me feel justified, not guilty, because at least I am facing up to the truth of how the meat on the supermarket shelves gets there. I might also add it is very rapidly turning me into a vegetarian.

Hesper gets starving hungry very quickly, in fact instantaneously, the moment she brings up a pellet. She can make the most extraordinarily wide gape when she swallows — she eats everything whole, without chewing or tearing of any sort, just straight down the hatch in a series of gulps, the final gulp, the one which administers the coup-de-grâce, being accompanied by a startled look, and then a rather choked smirk of complacency. The size of the stuff she can swallow is amazing. Now and then I give her a bigger bit than most, usually when she is ravenous and shrieking. The hisses reach a frantic crescendo as you approach, then she grips the piece of meat, grips it again, sort of throwing it in her mouth, experimenting for the best line of approach. When she is happy that she has got the angle correct given the size, shape and various protuberances of her supper, she throws her head back, grips again, throws it back, grips again, and bit by bit the thing vanishes down her throat.

She can swallow virtually half a chick whole. This is roughly the equivalent of a man sitting down to a meal of roast chicken, and picking up the bird — chestnut stuffing, bread sauce, bacon, brussel sprouts, roast potatoes and all — and swallowing the entire lot in a single gulp. And then digesting it.

Once the meal's gone down, she will go on calling for food for a few seconds more, even if she is full up, but she won't eat, just plays with the stuff and drops it. The tone of her calls has changed — the note of hysteria vanishes as soon as she is full, and now her voice grows softer and softer, until she usually reverts to her lovely, low, sweet, bubbling call.

Now she stands, beak sunk on her breast, looking extraordinarily reposeful and happy. Her feet are set out in that perfect star-shape. Her claws are extremely long and thin and needle-sharp like hypodermics. Round her ankle she wears her charm bracelet, her identity bracelet, showing she was bred in captivity. It can only be slipped over the foot when the owlet is around 10 days old — earlier than that it will just fall off, too late and it will be impossible to get on. This bracelet is with Hesper for life.

Now that she is spending more of her time standing up, perhaps she will get rid of those dreadful bald patches on the back of her legs where she has been squatting on her haunches.

Bits of white fluff are drifting off her, pushed out by the steady growth of the new feathers. I go and try and tempt her with a chick's head, but even though she's making a racket she doesn't really want it — she takes it from me, drops it, I pick it up, she nibbles it, sort of fondles it with her beak as if reluctant to refuse it, then drops it again. I pick it up and remove it — 'I'm not playing with a severed head all day'. There are times when the gore-fest becomes horribly amusing, such as when she ate the bottom half (tailless) of a small mouse, and it was like a little pair of mouse breeches were in her mouth, with two little mouse feet sticking out on either side.

24th May

The rain's knocked off most of the may blossom, and the round petals lie on the paths like the paper circles from a hole-punch, the remnants of some debauched office party. It's been drenched damp warm weather recently, heavy with the scent of may, gigantic slugs oozing everywhere with immense snot-coloured dignity and calm. Now it's got colder again, been raining on and off today.

Still keeping watch on the kestrels' nest. It looks splendid, fortress-like now, with the flowering horse-chestnuts with their huge creamy flowers and the immense tall trees heavy with rich foliage. The kestrels have a favourite dead branch where they perch, keeping watch over their domain — one day the male, the following day the female with a very baleful expression, staring down so arrogantly and so sternly that I decided to walk on. It was quite by accident that I discovered where they were nesting — I just happened to come down the field edge when one of the parents went in to feed the babies — I did not see anything, just heard the frenzied cheeping which I recognised from the kestrel at Alan's. It was very exciting to hear it after I had seen the parent birds hunting in the fields for two months.

It is because of the kestrels that I finally took the plunge and went on the falconry course at Alan's.

I had done the two days' falconry at Gleneagles in September, and after that I couldn't get the thought of the hawks out of my mind. My feelings about falconry were decidedly ambiguous, but one thing was for sure — those first two days had stuck with me — I just couldn't shake the memory off.

I read all the books I could get hold of, I bought everything I could on the subject. It began to madden me, that insane compulsion to keep on reading about falcons, eagles, hawks and owls, because the reading never got me any closer to making a decision. There were just too many damn questions. Would I dare? Could I do the unthinkable? Accept the responsibility of a bird of my own? And if so, what type? Harris hawks were easy but unspectacular-looking. Kestrels were too small. Eagles were too large. Buzzards were too lazy. Red-tails were too bolshy. Tawny owls were too difficult to get hold of. Barn owls were too fragile, or too dozy, or too boring, or some silly combination of all three. There were a thousand and one objections to every type of diurnal and nocturnal raptor — in other words it was much easier to just keep on reading.

The reading had acquired its own momentum. I was like a compulsive gambler or alcoholic — I couldn't stop myself acquiring more and more books on the subject, and getting more and more paralysed with indecision.

One day in March I took the dogs out for a walk. As I went down the sloping path towards Birch Wood, all those damned pestering annoying and depressing questions were whirling like a cloud of midges round my head. I said to myself, in melodramatic mood, 'Shall I or shan't I take up falconry? Will it or won't it be my salvation in life?' And then making the usual cry for help to a nonexistent deity, the sort of plea which has always fallen on resolutely stony ears in the past, I cried 'Give me a sign, Lord, give me a sign'.

What happened next was magical. Right on cue a kestrel flew down into the grass less than thirty feet away from me. I had never been so close to one before, nor had I ever seen one come down to earth as this one did. I've lived here for six and a half years and I never saw a kestrel in this field before that day. The kestrel did not seem bothered by me or the dogs. It was evidently searching for something. It flew up a few inches above the grass, and swept slowly up to the top of the hill where it dived again. Again it came up, and angled up into a holly bush at the edge of the wood, where it stayed for a few moments before flying off. I was amazed, stunned and delighted.

Commonsense came back, of course, after the initial thrill and rapture, and I decided this sign from God was just a freak and a coincidence. Still it was very odd. And divine guidance or not, it pleased me very much, so much so that I thought 'Yes, okay, it's enough — what more do I need? —

I've decided.' The next day, however, walking the dogs in the same field, I couldn't resist the temptation to cry out in a whiny spoilt kid kind of way, 'Lord, Lord, I can't be certain. Please give me another sign.' And the kestrel appeared again, this time darting swift as an arrow out of the wood, over my head and away.

I went back home, phoned Alan's, and booked my course.

I saw the kestrel several times after that: once blading up into a dead tree with an almost disdainful flick of its wings — it wasn't going to do anything so undignified and declassé as flapping; once dashing through the field brake on the edge of our garden (it was just a blur but I recognised that wonderful old-rose tint to its brownness); once hovering, silhouetted against the sky above the field, its tail spread out like a fan.

One rainy afternoon, it flew low across the grass again and landed on the single tree left in the field, a large oak. It perched on a knotty protuberance very close to the trunk, and sat there watching me, quite motionless. It was a misty greyish morning, a dull sort of light in between bouts of fine drifting rain. I did not want the bird to know I was watching in case I startled it away, so I carried on walking, not looking where I was going, my eyes intently fixed on the bird. Bit by bit as I moved, it vanished behind the trunk, and then as I went up the field, and gradually round the tree, so it slowly reappeared again. My eyes were so concentrated on that single beautiful motionless bird on the oak that, when at last I stopped still, the whole landscape went on wheeling and spinning around me, its anchor that one fixed spot.

The falcon tolerated the gawping maniac for a little longer, and then flew off.

Hesper is now 44 days old, or six and a half weeks. She

continues to develop at an exponential rate — she seems to change by the hour — the rate of development is staggering. She's improving in looks too, I'm sure. Brenda said 'It's rather better-looking this week, isn't it?' to which there could only be one answer — 'Well, there was only room for improvement'.

The network of feathers is shooting out ever more extensively under the fluff — there are masses of these tiny naked quills zig-zagging everywhere; they don't look real, more like the nylon fixings for artificial fur, a blown-up version of what you see on the flip side of fake fur coats. She's still covered in an unglamorous off-white, but there are real barn owl wing tips now appearing at the very end of her wings, the characteristic gorgeous gold-buff with its lacing of silver spots, really beautiful. There are other patches beneath the fluff of what appears to be perfect plumage, but when you part the frizz and examine it, it is nothing like as good — rather patchy and gappy, a perfect bit and then a missing bit, all in clumps. Her face is as grubby and weevil-like as ever, but she's a charmer alright — that wonderful melodious chitter so unlike how one would imagine an owl would speak. She still spends a lot of time admiring her splendiferous star-shaped feet. She tried to catch them yesterday, and became incredibly bemused by the fact they were always one step ahead of her, running away as soon as she moved.

Another characteristic pose is that of her beak sunk on her breast, her eyes staring straight down the beak as if admiring her own excellence, particularly the little puffed-up chest.

She is apt to get rather histrionic when removed from the cage when it has to be cleaned. The chittering revs up several knots.

It is when she's silent (which is very rare) that one can be alarmed, particularly by the bizarre postures that she strikes. Several times in the first few days that she was here I went in, saw her crashed out, neck at a stupendously unnatural angle, and thought 'Jesus Christ, that's it, she's snuffed it.' Now I just take her contortionist sleeping postures for granted. Other people who see her for the first time find it just as disconcerting as I used to. Kristine came into me in a state of mild alarm, and said 'Jennie, I don't want to worry you but the owl seems to be lying on its back'. 'Oh, it's nothing to worry about — that's what they do.' A secret thrill at uttering those blasé knowledgeable words for the first time.

Brenda said it reminded her of when her son Stephen was born, and how she kept having to go in to check that he was still breathing. It obviously reminded Bob of Stephen as well, as he took one look at Hesper and said 'It's just like Stephen as a baby — horrible to look at'.

I still do have the odd fit of panic when I think I'm going to go in and find her dead. A basic terror of birds' fragility is what has kept me from owning a bird for years — I've always loved parrots, for example, but could never summon up the courage to buy one.

My paranoia about birds' capacity for snuffing it came from a green budgerigar I had when I was 7 years old. She was called (to my huge grown-up embarrassment) Topsy.

Topsy was a gloomy peevish creature whose main pleasure in life was biting me. But I loved her. One evening she was rather poorly. I felt most sympathetic and concerned for her, and decided that I would keep her in my room all night, so that I could comfort and reassure her if she needed me. When I went to bed I placed her cage on the chair right next to my pillow. In the morning I awoke and my first sight was of Topsy lying flat on her back on the floor of her cage, her little grey feet scrunched up, pointing almost accusingly at the sky. When I got her out, I could feel that loathsome mortician's chill right through her soft feathers. She was very cold and strangely stiff, hollow and inanimate like a roll of cardboard. She was dead, alright — she couldn't have got much deader. I was completely and absolutely shattered.

Her death permanently put the blight on any vision of myself as a natural healer of wild life. In later years, whenever I tried to succour the injured wild birds I came across, I discovered I lacked the Saint Francis touch as spectacularly as ever. Buddy was my first success story, Buddy the flightless crow whom I've had for over a year now.

As for Hesper, though she seems so immensely fragile, it is obvious that in her own way she is as tough as old boots, her grip on life thoroughly tenacious. The only mild sign of her fragility has been one or two upset stomachs, none lasting longer than a couple of hours. The first time I panicked — diarrhoea, death, melodrama, and so on. Was it the wrong food, the right food at the wrong temperature, too much food, too little food, food full of bugs, a stomach chill, a disease, a congenital malformation? Though it was, probably, her change of address, she has given no particular indication of that upsetting her — indeed she has been completely and comically laid back about the move. She has not turned a hair at the dogs, probably because there were three at Alan's, and she takes no interest in the cats either.

All in all, she is remarkably relaxed about everything. Nothing much seems to upset her — she is amiable, friendly, and interested in what goes on around her in a fairly easy sort of way. She likes being gently scratched about the gills, but is not fond of being picked up, she starts chittering loudly and quickly 'Oh, I don't like that — put me down, put me down'. But even here she adapts quickly, and yesterday submitted to being carried about quite a bit and plonked on the carpet in a strange room, then on a table next to the ornate candlesticks, and finally being posed on the carved African box — all this in the line of a photocall, to capture her endearing hideousness before it completely vanishes. She showed virtually no signs of nervousness. The flashlight of the camera, which blinks rapidly and makes a little rattle of clicking noises before it goes off, attracted her attention every time, but she just looked astonished and very curious — there was not the least taint of fear. We took her out in the garden for five minutes, and though she was obviously much more startled by the huge space round her and the stunning sunlit brightness of it, yet she stood up bravely and brightly and just looked around her. The only sign of nerves she betrayed was when Jon was holding her in a cack-handed way, not the correct procedure of hands round wings and fingers laced beneath her belly, and she caught onto the material of his trousers with her claws, as if to stop herself from falling.

Hesper doesn't have the constant human need for eye contact. She hears you, talks to you, but doesn't often bother to look round if she is facing the other way and you arrive and start speaking to her. Even when you shout out 'Oy! 'Ere! Hesp!' she doesn't bother herself to turn round though she may very well be hissing ferociously for food. When the meal comes, she makes no effort to locate it for herself or to adjust her posture in any way — it's up to you to steer it over her shoulders, to touch the sensitive whiskers on either side of her beak, and nine times out of ten these contortions merely lead to the meat being dropped in the bedclothes where it stays until you retrieve it. Eventually, however, she gets the thing in her beak, and then there's the characteristic blinking astounded gulp as she swallows it down.

For the first time today I saw her give a sort of shaking motion of the head as she took the meat, the same sort of determined violent shake a dog gives when it is trying to break its victim's neck. Was this the same thing, a reflex action, an instinct to demolish any last resistance in the prey?

Hesper does very well in human company, as in their own particular way wild barn owls have done for centuries. Barn owls have always lived very close to man, using buildings for nest sites, hunting round the hayricks and grainstacks for mice. They were familiar sights to country people, and their folk names show how affectionately they were regarded — Old Hushwing, Billy Wise, Billy Wix, Gill Howter, Jenny Howlet, Jenny Owl, Moggy, Padge, Pudge, Oolert, Woolert, Owlerd, Roarer, Gillihowlett, Gil-hooter.

It's a great pity that the name the owl is known by nowadays is the horribly lumpy and unpoetic 'Barn' Owl. How much nicer if it had kept one of its other names — the White Owl (like its Latin name, Tyto Alba), or the very beautiful and haunting Cherubim or Church Owl.

It has also been called the Screech Owl, Scrich Owl or Scritch Owl, referring to their cry — they don't hoot, but apparently give a tremendous, piercing and very menacing scream. It has also been called the Yellow Owl, the Silver Owl, the Screaming Owl. 'The Hissing Owl' is even more appropriate.

Owls, of which there are 133 different species in the world, are classified as the order Strigiformes. This has two main families, Strigidae and Tytonidae. Tytonidae, the one I'm concerned with, contains two subfamilies, the single genus *Tyto* (barn and grass owls) and the single genus *Phodilus* (bay owls — I seem to remember a bay owl is a sort of weird insect catcher, who flies about with its mouth gaping open like those whales who sieve whole oceans for plankton).

Tyto is an amazingly old race. It is difficult to comprehend quite how ancient it is — it had been on the planet for *nineteen and a half million years* before mankind even began to dream of bestowing names upon it. The oldest modern owls, eagle and eared, are thought to have been in their present form for around 35 million years. As relative newcomers, the white owls first appeared about 20 million years ago. First true man, Homo sapiens, came a mere 500,000 years ago, and had a stupendous amount of mental aerobics to struggle through before he was capable of classifying anyone.

People who have anything to do with owls usually remark laughingly how stupid the birds are. Stupidity, however, is strictly relative. As a race, owls are amazingly successful. If the human race lasts for 20 million years, a thoroughly unlikely proposition, then it can talk about owls being stupid.

May 25th

We went to Howlett's Farm yesterday, where they have various rare breeds of animals. There were dozens — in fact far too many — sheep and goats crammed in the tiny paddocks — there is a major problem with dung, all shapes and sizes of it, and very much in evidence. I'm bored by sheep and goats — that's what I mean by far too many — they are creatures I find it difficult to like. There was one odd bunch of sheep which appeared to be self-shearing, and who walked about with vast bald unsightly patches and huge wodges of wool peeling off them. A group of them sat under the shelter (it kept raining, in little windy showers) and chewed away frenetically, bearing a very striking resemblance to American baseball managers and reserves, sitting on the sidelines, watching their team play — the same rapidly circulating jaws, vacant faces and glazed expressions — only the baseball caps were missing.

The bird life was more exciting, a very glam show-off peacock, who kept posing everywhere, and some exquisite Gold Lace Wyndotte bantams, the hens very prettily marked with little dark arrowheads on a gold background, the cocks the usual resplendent symphony of metallic greens, coppers, blacks and vermillions. We went to ask if they had any for sale, but they didn't and said to ring back later in the summer.

Round the back of the farm was a woodland walk and a couple of murky pools, with starving wild fowl in them. We threw them the corn we had bought at an extortionate price with the entry tickets.

In the wood there was a reconstruction of an Iron Age house, a large round pitch-dark hut with no windows, a thatched roof and an earthen floor. As a home in those far-off days, it was probably very snug and warm when the fire was lit. And also probably blinding with smoke and horribly infested with fleas and body lice. Pulmonary diseases, bronchitis, pneumonia, tuberculosis, ague, rheumatism, arthritis, rotten teeth, death from simple accidents because they would bring septicaemia or gangrene, all the lovely enchantments of a world without doctors, dentists or hospitals. And yet I can't help in some way envying such a life, truly part of the natural world, separated from it only by the thinnest of skins, in touch with sunset and sunrise, and hearing all the sounds of the night, not isolated and kept away from them by solid brick walls and tiled roofs.

27th May

The Hespernelli noise factor has been getting out of hand — in fact she should be called Hisspernelli. She seems to be a bit peevish at the moment, and has replaced that delightful chittering noise with constant loud hissing like a pit of vipers with laryngitis, *definitely not* an improvement. Jon's been getting irritated, and the other night banished her from the sitting room because he could not hear the television properly. Now she starts up at breakfast whilst we're in the kitchen and he goes 'Shut up, shut up', not particularly vehemently but obviously not in the least bit amused by it.

Hesper and her accoutrements are out of favour altogether. I get a mouse out for her breakfast, go off for five minutes to do something else, and when I come back find Jon irritably clearing up the breakfast things by the side of the sink. He points to the mouse, a white one, very limp, very dejected, and very dead, lying amongst the cups and plates.

Jon: [Crossly] Do you want that?
Me: Yes, I do. I'm tidying up in here. Leave it alone. Go away.
Jon: Fuck off then.
Me: Fuck off yourself.

The usual erudite matrimonial exchange that we go in for.

White mouse vanishes — peace is restored — but Jon quits the kitchen to find silence elsewhere.

So Jon's out of love with the baby now. There will be no more dandling over the foetid cradle, cooing endearments in a high-pitched soppy voice. Shameful though it is to admit it, we've both been doing this, and now I think it's time to drop it, because I've begun to realise how grossly inappropriate it is for an owlet. The natural human instinct, when faced with a tiny creature, is to pet it, to stroke it, to babble nonsense at it, to constantly touch and make contact with it, seeking by such physical handling to comfort and reassure the lost little thing. It is patently obvious that the owl doesn't need this. She likes company, but she does not crave it, nor does she need to be petted — a little scratch, a little playful dabbling around the gills are the limits of the caresses she requires. And even that is often too much — when I played the scratching game today, she bit my hand crossly, as if to say 'That's enough there. Clear orf.'

It occurs to me that the appearance of ill-humour she has suddenly taken on may be due to boredom, so I carry her out to the aviary in a cardboard box for a couple of hours, half in the sun and half in the shade. She makes a miserable little cheeping at first, looks very forlorn, then her usual equanimity takes over and she's fine. So perhaps she wants more stimulation now she's getting a bit older. For example, she was perfectly happy last night in the sitting room when I set her right next to the window — she stood bolt upright, watching the darkening garden, bobbing her head up and down and from side to side as she spotted strange alien shapes and shadows in the night. She was almost completely silent — a little chirrup now and then — none of that perpetual aggravating hissing.

What has also improved her temper is giving her a whole mouse to play with, instead of the usual cut-up pieces. A couple of the mice in the new batch were so small that it seemed quite feasible for her to devour them in one piece so I chose the smallest and laid it in the furthest corner of her tray. (She still lives in the parrot cage, but most of the time the top part, the structure of bars, is removed.) Hesper turned round, and, unusually for her, spotted the food straightaway. She walked across to the mouse determinedly, with that funny half run, half strut she has, and picked it up and took it back to her bed. It was clear that she had recognised the mouse shape instantly (even though it is highly unlikely she has ever seen a whole mouse before but only the various disparate parts) and it was also evident that she was delighted with her treasure. She played with it for quite a while, constantly nibbling it, almost caressing it with her beak, holding it with one foot bunched up and trying very ineffectually to tear it — all she succeeded in doing was stretching it like a bit of elastic. The movements were all very gentle and rather inept, but it seems she knows instinctively what to do. When she is older, she will dismember her food herself, she will make an entry point in the hide and from there eat out the insides, but at the moment she does not have the power to do this. She has no alternative but to swallow it whole. Finally, after about half an hour, she brought herself to this point, a big effort, because even once she had got the bulk of the mouse down, still its long tail protruded from her beak. That was a bit of a poser — she went on nibbling on the tail, like a man chewing on a cigar — then at last she gave a series of gulps and managed to get that down as well.

She's looking more grown-up than ever. In certain lights you can see a sort of vivid golden haze behind the fluff as if she's glowing underneath it. The discarded bits of this baby feathering are becoming more and more plentiful, drifting about like snowflakes when she indulges in a vigorous piece of flapping — she flapped so hard this afternoon that she almost took off. The primary feathers look fully formed, but they're still a bit ragged when you get a close look at them, perfect patches here and there, then a break, then another bit which is perfect, then another break — this along the length of each quill so that the effect is a bit like topiary or poodle-trimming, as if someone has deliberately clipped and shaped it.

I forgot to say about the mouse thing — the whole mouse entire — that when I gave her another later in the day, she didn't appear to recognise it in the same way. The first mouse was dark, the second mouse was white. She completely ignored the white mouse, didn't seem to see it as the same as the first, or perhaps it blended in more with the white of the newspaper on which it was lying. Seems an unlikely theory. I'll try with another white mouse tomorrow.

28th May

White mouse experiment in progress at the moment. Hesper seems more interested in watching me write, bobbing her head from side to side in that extremely delightful and endearing way owls have, her eyes round and bright with astonishment. Now she's gone back to staring out of the window at the garden, which is a source of endless fascination to her. She saw collared doves, wood pigeons and squirrels on the lawn this morning, eating the wild bird food I put out each day. She did not approve of the squirrels at all and started clopping her beak at them.

Her coordination has improved immensely, her rate of progress is almost unbelievable — if I went away for a day or two, I would miss an awful lot, because she is virtually changing by the hour. It is only two days since she managed to hold something properly with her foot for the first time. She grabbed a piece of meat and it was obviously a very satisfying moment for her, she was eyeing her foot clenched about the scrap — it was still on the floor, she had not carried it up to her beak like a parrot, such a skill will come later. She bobbed her head this way and that, regarding her own cleverness, then she tried to get hold of the meat with the other foot as well, not having grasped the principle that you need a minimum of one foot to stand on, staggered and fell down on her bottom.

I'm very happy just sitting here, taking notes and watching Hesp out of the corner of my eye. Went through a period on Friday when I suddenly had an intense desire to give up the whole thing. It was the Quease Factor, a culmination of all the nausea and revulsion I feel over preparing her food. Decided I would get a nice seed-eating bird instead, something which didn't demand I plunged up to the elbows in blood, preparing her hideous gore-fests at the fell hour of midnight. Decided it was all an immense mistake, and that an African Grey parrot would do a lot better, or perhaps, if I wanted to be flamboyant, something insane like a Scarlet Macaw.

It had been the last straw when the consignment of Hesper's meat arrived at lunchtime on Friday. Never having ordered a batch before, I was unsure of how much room it would take up in the fridge, but the carriage charges are so expensive it would be uneconomic to buy little and often, so I over-ordered. Horribly. When the stuff arrived, packed in wadding and newspaper but already wet, soggy and a bit defrosted about the edges, I realised I had nowhere to put it. It was a moment of unadulterated horror, surrounded by eighty quidsworth of cadavers, all in a critical stage of meltdown, metamorphosing gradually with each minute that passed into a puddle of bloody icewater mixed with carnage.

Had to take everything out of the large icebox of our fridge — fishfingers, bread, stuffing for the turkey, tuna fish spread, fishcakes, breast of chicken, etc, and stuff in the bags of owl food instead. There was one bag of mice which was too far gone — this had to be kept out of the freezer and stored in the bottom part of the fridge instead. The whole fridge/freezer seemed to be seething, writhing, squeaking and wailing with accusatory corpses — mice tails everywhere, floppy droopy chicks, and stuffed right at the back (I haven't even dared to look at them) twenty quails in full set of feathers. I am not all partial to the idea of having my own dinner, teas, & co, mixed up with owl fodder, which will never have been handled with the strict attention to hygiene demanded where human foodstuffs are concerned. Felt disgusted to an even more extreme degree than normal.

Got everything stashed away at last, but the fishfingers, stuffing, etc, went to the crows once defrosted — they obligingly cleared them all off the lawn within five minutes of me setting the feast out. I continued, however, to feel really septic about the whole business, and when I went to bed, in that black and midnight mood where all life seems one sordid gloomy nightmare, I resolved that I would have NO MORE OWLS.

In the bright light of morning, of course, all was transformed and I realised that rather than my life with Hesper being a total tragedy all I had to do was to buy another fridge.

Hesper's sussed the white mouse now, so bang goes that theory. She picked it up about ten minutes ago, and played with it on and off between long sessions of staring intently out of the window. Even as I watch her, she starts yawning, a prodigious yawn, then another even more cadaverous. Her head is in profile and I can perfectly see her hooked beak like a witch's and the quite amazingly long, thin, sharp, pink tongue she has. Up comes a pellet without the least appearance of effort or straining — it's not like us being sick, a sequence of profound muscular spasms, but as airy as letting out a small aspiration of breath. Even a human hiccup or belch seems more effort — Hesper's pellet just slides obligingly up and out. Instantly she picks up the mouse again, with vastly increased interest, shakes it about like a little dog, then drops it and picks up the pellet. I consider removing the pellet in case she eats it, but no, after a minute or two of tapping it about in her beak she drops it and picks up the mouse once more. She starts the preliminary beak shuffle to manoeuvre it into place. I feel smugly and confidently assured that she will swallow it as she had done all the others, nose first, then body, then tail. This is the correct barn owl method of procedure, I'm convinced. Instead just to contradict all I've written in my notebook, Hesper attempts to swallow the mouse *sideways*, bunched up lengthways across her jaws, a seemingly impossible feat. It won't go in. Ah hah, I think, now she'll rearrange it properly. But she just sort of bunches it up a bit more, victim's head tucked into victim's shoulder, victim's tail wrapped around victim's body, takes a determined gulp — half in — takes another — and it's gone. She recommences scanning the garden, with an occasional break for what Eddie calls 'pruning her feathers'.

I've been writing up these notes for two and a half hours, sitting right next to her — I'm on the sofa, she's on the carved African box in her own private suite, but all the time I am writing I'm stopping to watch her. It's difficult to explain the fascination of her. The hours just float airily past, one after another like clouds in the sky, and I never get bored. It's strange really, because it's not as if she does that much — her repertoire contains only a very limited number of variables — hissing (at which she is expert); walking very badly; performing stretching exercises; eating; excreting; tidying her feathers; sleeping in amazing postures where she's sprawled out and looks like a chicken that's been run over, an avian pancake with bright eyes and a single leg with great insouciance sticking out the rear. I've seen everything that she does many times, but firstly the uncanny speed with which she is changing is so fascinating; secondly however ugly she remains she is still extraordinarily endearing — she is comical and charming and delightful — she is the ultimate specialist in 'cute'.

She flaps her wings very strongly now and it's like Christmas — little bits of snow whirl everywhere. All of a sudden her wings have got so long that they make a little ping against the bars of the cage. The bars are only replaced at night now, to protect her from danger. She spends most of her days in here, in her tray in the sitting room, with the door firmly shut against feline marauders. If you walk past outside you can sometimes see her looking out. The window's raised up about seven feet above ground level, and there you spy this tiny little white figure, bolt-upright, staring out at you with great, wide, round, black eyes. She looks exceptionally pretty like that, a miniature abominable snowman, standing all straight and motionless, pure white. And then all of a sudden she blinks, and these enormous filmstar eyelashes sweep down — she is the very incarnation of Hollywood glamour.

Mostly however, she leaves the glamour stuff well alone. Oh Little Stinky Primaeval One.

1st June

The last few days have been taken up with the builders — moving all the stuff out of the basement, finding space for it upstairs, dealing with them and their works. Battering-ram drill and clouds of dust for the first two days, then silence fell apart from odd sloshing, slapping, seeping and banging noises.

As for the builders themselves, they have an uncanny knack of appearing the moment I walk up the garden path, a dead mouse swinging by its tail from my hand. The fridge/freezer now temporarily in the summerhouse, stuffed full with its charnel load of mice, chicks and quails, so I'm sneaking my booty back to the house to feed the hissing monster and hoping that no one's going to catch me at it. Normal people just don't go in for this sort of thing. The other day Mr Talbot, the boss, asked to speak to me, and I had to close my mitt round the latest cadaver, a small white mouse with lovely pink nose and tail, a pretty little thing which later went down Hesper's gullet in five seconds flat. It's a bit like being a serial killer, transporting the bodies in this secretive way. Everyone goes all soft and sentimental over the mice — even Bob, an ex-butcher, went 'Poor Little Micky' when he saw one lying at Hesper's feet. So me and Hesp have got to keep our nasty habits secret.

No great changes in Hesper since I last wrote these notes,

just more of the same — wing-stretching, feather-preening, food-stuffing, hissing. But she is all of a sudden growing really really pretty — at certain times, in particular moods and lights, she is absolutely dazzling and beguiling. Her eyes seem to have become huger and brighter — they often appeared to have a dullish sheen before, but now they are magnificent — alert, bright, blazing, inquisitive, intelligent, immense. Her whole face has changed, the ravaged physiognomy has disappeared and instead you have this enchanting little phiz, round and very soft-looking, as cute as cute can be. It is snow-white with pretty pale buff accentuation marks at the eyes and beak. The skull shape of the facial disk has changed to a heart shape, created by the stiff ruff that stands out all around. The top of the ruff is now developing the characteristic adult gold-buff tint. And since I've started feeding her whole mice, the congealed breakfast-in-the-whiskers element has gone, which is a very considerable augmentation to her beauty.

Her wing tips show all the time now, no longer partially concealed by fluff. They are exquisite, golden-buff mottled with dark iron-grey with tiny silver stars and droplets to vary them, and pure white scallops to some of the edges. Her baby fluff remains covering her body but it is evidently lying only on the surface of what is virtually a complete set of adult feathers. As the fluff has thinned out, so it has lost that nasty medical off-white, and has become true white, especially on the underparts where the adult feathers are a delicious moonbeam silver. Her legs are clad in pure white fluff too, so that she looks very lushly dressed, rather eighteenth century pageboy. She really is looking delicious.

It's curious how deceptive photographs can be — those taken of very young owlets by no means capture their true nightmarish hideousness, whilst those taken of Hesper's current age make them look like rather nasty ragbags, their adult feathers jumbled on any old how and bits of fungoid fluff sprouting everywhere. Actually in real life this effect is very charming.

Even her tail is growing at last, miles after her wings (which are evidently much more complicated, much harder work) so that ridiculous little stump looks a little more elegant and a little less like a roast chicken's rump.

She constantly nibbles her feathers up and down, and has now perfected the difficult art of drawing out a feather through her beak, the skilful movement unzipping and rezipping the interlocking barbs. When she's taking a rest from her work of tidying, she flaps her wings with energetic enthusiasm — this raises a great gale and blizzards of snow, but does not actually lift her off the ground. She's preening now, and as she does so she utters a constant contented little hiss, nothing like the rasping hectoring racket which assails you if you go near her when she wants grub — this is rather the barn owl equivalent of humming.

All this feather-growing work, its constant itching and disturbance to her skin, have made her tetchy, because she definitely doesn't like being touched at the moment and chitters very scoldingly when you do. She'll bite if you persist, start clattering that pale ivory-rose hook and if you don't move quickly you're stapled.

(As I scribble away in my notebook, I can hear the two peacocks up at the farm howling away to each other across the shallow valley — they sound like two camp actors using a megaphone and impersonating a cat being tortured — meow, MeoWW, MEOOOWWWW.)

The funniest thing that Hesper does is the cartoon double-take on a mouse. You lay the treat down and it may be a few seconds before she spots it — when she does she starts back, the very picture of ravaged astonishment and amazement. 'Good God, what is that? Can it be? No, surely not. I must be seeing things.' She violently shakes her head to dispel the illusion. The illusion remains, however, and now, gathering confidence that the thing really exists, she begins to bob and duck her head, really swinging it from side to side to get a look at it from every possible angle. As she becomes more certain, the movements lose their exaggerated quality, and when at last she's convinced beyond all doubt, she stomps over to get it with great determination and stomps back to eat it in bed.

I love to see her in the classic barn owl pose, standing on one leg, one foot tucked into the puffed silvery down of her breast, dozing meditatively, beak down, eyes three-quarters closed. She looks incredibly pretty like this. She almost invariably adopts this pose when she's watching out of the window, sort of drops off in mid-stare and snoozes upright. If you walk by outside she wakes up in an instant, her eyes all bright and huge with wonderment and amazement though she clearly knows it is me. I wave and act preposterous and she watches me with mild amusement, a little bolt-upright snowman with black button eyes.

Sleeping like this is a far more elegant business than when she adopts the raffish lying-down posture. Sometimes, crashed out, but still hissing and staring round as if her neck is dislocated, she actually looks worried and harassed for once, an extremely rare thing with her, a sort of its-all-too-much-for-me expression. Jon has taken to referring to her as The Cowpat when she lies sprawled out like this. When I ask him to justify this unkind remark, he says she is just like a large fluffy cowpat with eyes.

3rd June

Hesper is 54 days old. After anxiously consulting my book, I've decided she is making slow progress in the accomplishment line. According to the sage, at 50 days the tail feathers are longer than the primaries (eh what? no way. Can this be the same type of bird we're talking about?), and the owlet is making its first attempt at flight.

At 56 days, it will be following its mother around in the vicinity of the nest site and learning hunting techniques. The way the mother owl teaches her young to hunt is to fly around outside the nest site, in circles, with food in her talons, calling to the owlets to come out and gorge themselves. When she has an audience arranged to her satisfaction, some on the ground, the more advanced ones flying, and all no doubt hissing like a batch of crazed snakes, she deliberately drops the meal. There is a free-for-all — some try to catch it in mid-air, but usually nobody gets it and it falls to the ground. The advanced siblings then hover about, attempting to locate it, and the retarded ones dive into the grass and search.

At 70 — 77 days, the first prey catch is made, and the first pure screech is heard.

We show no signs whatsoever of preparing for anything so exhausting and energetic.

I get Hesper out of the tray and put her on the carpet on the sitting room floor. We've got to get this program moving somehow.

Hesper freezes and remains stock-still, as if flabbergasted. I can see that she is staring at the skirting board with a manic, fixed and piercing glare. I look at the skirting board. It is a very boring skirting board. It has no moulding to it, no unusual features of any sort, and it is painted in an ancient white gloss with the sole embellishment of having a couple of chips out of it. It is a deep mystery as to what is exciting Hesper's possible fear and wrath. She stares and stares and stares and stares. I lie down on the carpet next to her, getting down to her level, but still I can't spot the mesmerising attraction of it.

It is the first time I've been this close to her for longer than a minute or so. For the first time I perceive she has a particular faint smell, a pale odour which is vaguely suggestive of church mould, tombs, old flower water, mustiness, the grave, sacred buildings long unaired. It's a strange little perfume, unexpected, and I'm not quite sure whether it is agreeable or not.

Hesper accepts quite unconditionally me lying next to her at full length on the floor, though it seems she's never realised before quite how ridiculously long I am. She has stopped scrutinising the skirting board now, and is looking around at everything else, and occasionally she bobs and dips to get me all in, my long weird unconscionable sprawl. At last she starts to move, one or two of her favourites hops, unaccompanied by much in the way of wing power — she jumps with both feet together about three inches into the air, with a look of great pride in her athletic skill and judgement, but there is not the remotest chance of her actually getting airborne.

Now she stomps across to the edge of the carpet and onto the parquet surround. The different surface doesn't seem to upset her much — it's rough old stuff, not too slippery or shiny for claws. She investigates the doorstop and the corner of the wicker basket, then does a very large and very wet shit, pumping it out, flapping her wings to keep herself still and give the ejection real force. The only good thing about this is that she has helpfully aimed it at the parquet not the carpet, so it only takes half a minute to clear up.

She chitters anxiously as I go out to get the cloth, but her usual placid temperament is foremost and she doesn't seem particularly fazed. She ignores it completely when I vanish briefly for a second time to return the cloth to the kitchen.

Thinking there can't be any more accidents just yet, I

settle down comfortably to watch the show. But Hesper hasn't finished yet. She moves round the corner of the sofa, opens her mouth and does a large wet pellet. I decide to leave the pellet where it is for the time being.

Hesper now goes back to practising hopping. One, two, three, which takes her right up to the side of the sofa — she then carries on hopping *into* the sofa and bouncing back off it again, apparently not having grasped the true spiteful nature of solid objects, i.e. that they get in your way and stop you going somewhere.

Not particularly keen to have Hesper do something unspeakable to the sofa next, I put her on my lap. She walks up my trousers and onto my bare arm. Her claws are incredibly, unbelievably sharp, even though she's by no means digging them in, just resting them with a little curve on the skin. It's like being walked on by a bramble bush. I make a silent vow to be more toughly dressed next time.

I pull my sleeve down. Hesper obligingly moves onto sleeve, but I can still feel her needle-sharp talons through the material. I very very gently move my arm — this is what she will have to get used to when she's trained, so why not start now? Hesper allows me to move her quite graciously, though she chitters a little anxiously and scoldingly if I move too fast. Her faint tomblike smell rises in my nostrils. She's loving this — the excitement, doing something new. I put her back on the floor once more and move to the other side of the room, wondering if she'll be nervous because I've abandoned her in a strange place — not a bit of it — she doesn't care at all and goes off exploring behind a footstool.

I get a mouse and show it to her. Normally she would be going beserk for food after dropping a pellet, now she completely ignores it. I drag the mouse temptingly in front of her, then suddenly reflect that I don't particularly want mouse trails all over my carpet. I put the mouse in her tray.

Forty minutes have vanished like seconds already — I've a hundred other things to do and reluctantly I decide I must put her back in her tray. Yet I don't — I go on watching, entranced. I only terminate the experiment when she decides to explore the dark place behind the television, full of trailing wires and dust. I pick her up, she scolds me, but when I put her back in her tray on top of the African box she accepts it with perfect grace, only occasionally looking over the side a little longingly at the fascinating playground she's just left. She does not look at the little corpse beside her. The mouse lies untouched — even food briefly seems to have lost its overpowering allure. My arm feels as if it's been pricked all over by a manic doctor with a hypodermic syringe.

4th June

Continuing with the Hesper education program. I'm the mother owl, teaching her the ropes, but I'm also the annoying human who wants to inculcate the falconry principles early.

Having been used as a pincushion yesterday, I decide to try out my very expensive, very posh, very new falconry glove. It is pristine, has never been used before, is a vision of the softest palest golden buckskin with a gorgeous nap to it like velvet, a pendant tassel and an olive-green leather trim. I show this lovely creation to Hesper, wondering how soon she'll crap on it.

Living up to her nature, Hesper is entirely placid and unfazed by this new object — I try gently pushing it against the back of her legs and before I know it she's stepped onto it. Wow, this is it! It is a true moment of epiphany. Very very gently I raise her slowly out of her box. There is some nervous wing-flapping to help her keep her balance but more, I feel certain, because she has felt the sensation of movement than because she feels in any danger of falling. I have got her out now, I am kneeling, and I slink slowly down on my haunches, still holding the glove outstretched as steadily as possible. She is still a trifle unsteady and nervous, but now she begins to examine the glove and with a mild fractiousness to peck it.

The glove has been put to the test and has come up trumps — even though she gives my thumb a good bite I don't feel it other than a slight pinching pressure. Those fiendish hypodermic claws I don't feel at all. She seems perfectly calm, sitting there on the glove — I can tell the progress of her mood quite easily, by the companionable incessant hiss she makes, a sort of constant conversational gambit: 'I'm here — are you there?', repeated over and over again, a sound I find very pleasing. When she gets nervous, this sound changes to chitters, first a few little sprinkled notes, and then louder and more persistent as her fear or irritation grows. If I stop still, the chitters die down and cease, and are replaced by the low conversational hiss. In other words it's extremely easy to tell if I'm going too far too fast.

After a while, with extreme caution, I stand up, reach my full height, still with her perching on my hand. I make one or two very very abbreviated circuits of the room, at a stately creeping pace, as if I'm a hundred and ten years old. Then I judge that is enough for our first effort, and I return her to her box. Hesper, who is evidently extremely fascinated and intrigued by her outings, accepts this return to the nursery with perfect equanimity and recommences her favourite occupation of staring out of the window.

A sudden roll of thunder makes her jump, but she soon recovers herself and just looks curious. Now the storm breaks, and tumultuous torrential sheets of rain fall, thundering down, obscuring the garden in a vertical haze. The gutters of the house overflow, and the deluge starts pattering down the window at the side — this intrigues her very much. And still she is incredibly fascinated by the scratching movement of my pen. This strange companionship we've started to share — she obviously likes my presence — I really like hers — she has the most extraordinarily restful and peaceful effect. She is totally different from my dogs and cats, the mammals, with their high-wrought nervous tension and intelligence, their constant mental alertness and paranoia. Does she have to learn how to fear, how to be afraid, how to be sharp and on edge all the time? She gives no sign whatsoever of having that razor-sharp alertness a bird of prey of all beings in creation must surely have. Do I, as ersatz parent, have to teach her this? Do I have to teach her the meaning of fear? Nothing appears to feature as an enemy in her mind but ridiculous things like storm-tossed trees or chips out of a badly painted skirting board. That's hardly enough to get her safely through life. I'm acutely aware of her vulnerability, her fragility, her astonishing idiotic bravery. I guess her total unawareness of it is part of her mesmeric charm.

I said to Jon the other night that it was amazing what a happy little creature she was. 'I don't want her to live an unnatural life — well, it *is* unnatural but she doesn't seem the least bit bothered by it.' Considering 75% of all wild owlets die in their first year, I don't think Hesper is doing too badly in terms of lifestyle.

6th June

The ducklings have vanished off Flusher's Pond again this year. I saw them first around May 25th, eleven of them escorted by their very proud mother. It was a sunlit morning, very pleasant — they sailed along, in and out of the dappled pools of sunlight, little spotted golden-brown balls, an exquisitely beautiful sight. One little creature was chasing flies, rushing over the surface of the pond, light as a bubble, almost blown away by the speed of its own dash. It looked incredibly pretty and joyful. I haven't seen them since, despite going past every day. The pond has a scummy grey blear-eyed look — it looks empty and desolate without them. Two very handsome drakes there today, but no sign of the duck or any of her babies. Exactly the same thing happened last year. It's two years since there was a successful batch, again a brood of eleven, reduced down to five, all of which grew to maturity and flew off in the autumn.

There has been no sign of the kestrels either. I made the mistake of taking the binoculars up there last week, because every time I went by I saw one of the parent birds on their favourite dead branch. That particular morning, wanting to see them better, I lugged the heavy glasses up the hill, and of course neither of them were anywhere to be seen. Alarmingly, they have not been around since, and neither have I seen any of the young birds. It can't be easy for them, the farmer having ploughed up the two big fields surrounding their copse, which were home for many voles and mice. The cats were forever coming back here with their kills, littering the back door steps with their slaughter, including — on different occasions — a mole, a weasel and a stoat. Mostly they bring home shrews and mice, some of which are eaten on the back door mat, the neatly sliced-out organs which they don't want being abandoned. One organ is filled with green sludge — is it the spleen? — which of course makes a lovely veridian cowpat when you tread in it. The cats have fads for what they eat and what they reject: at one stage they always ate the heads and left the bodies; at another they ate the bodies and left the heads — one morning I came out and found four little mouse heads staked out on the mat spikes, the feline equivalent of Traitor's Gate.

Lushka, the red and white borzoi, caught a mouse in that field once, the only time she has ever caught anything. It was an extremely unlucky mouse, exactly in the wrong place at the wrong time. She stopped for a moment, and it rustled in the grass beneath her — perhaps she had actually trodden on it. The instant it moved it was doomed. With lightening quick reflexes, which seemed to amaze even her, Lushka snapped out. There was no time for considered thought — it was just a matter of instinct — she looked rather stunned by what happened next. The mouse had received a lethal chop to the neck, as clean as an axe blow to an ox, a deep v-shaped cut that had severed the spinal column. For five seconds or so, literally dying on its feet, it ran round in pitiful nightmarish little circles. Then it staggered, fell, lay still and moved no more. A very pretty little creature — its ill-considered death seemed sad somehow, and cast a melancholy shadow over the morning.

Hesper is not doing terribly well when I put her out each day in the aviary for an airing. Twice I've found her hiding behind the logs as if afraid. I've got to find some way of getting her happy in there really quickly, as we are going on holiday in three weeks and she really has to learn to be outside at night. It is an unspeakable temptation just to keep her indoors, but I realise once she learns to fly that will be impossible.

Having her so close to me each day, as we practise our walking-around-sitting-on-the-glove routine, I've seen that her eyes aren't uniform black at all but have the most incredible centres — darkest midnight blue with a sort of electric glow to them. They look like two stars shining in deep space, really beautiful. I only see this effect now and then when the light is falling from a particular angle.

Her ruff continues to develop with the rest of her feathers, and I see now quite how important its structure is — it was only hinted at before, sort of soft and wispy and insubstantial — now it is firming up, becoming more pronounced, bearing her little face on it as though on a plate. It has exactly the same effect as the ceremonial clothing in grand Elizabethan portraits, where the face sits in isolation, perfectly framed, on a circle of gorgeous stiff white lace.

Chapter Three - Independence

8th June

Two not very satisfactory days as far as aviary familiarisation is concerned. I set up a cardboard box, as Hesper appeared to be nervous about being out in the daylight, and she at once greeted this refuge with great relish. I set her down on the log which forms the grand entrance drive, she spotted the dark interior with glee, and immediately stomped off into it, not returning but responding to my attempts to lure her out with lots of little amiable twitterings and hissings. When I bent down to look in, there she was crouching, bobbing and dipping her head, perfectly happy to stay where she was. She did not come out until I went back later to collect her. This has been the pattern ever since. As long as I am in the aviary with her, she will stay out in the open, but the moment I leave she goes back into her little cave again. This entirely defeats the point of her being outside. She doesn't practise learning to fly in there, doesn't even bounce around flapping her wings and getting exercise — she saves all that up for when she's back indoors again, when her movements are inevitably restricted and she gets frustrated with being restrained.

The daring little skips, hops and jumps of about three or six inches at a time remain her sole accomplishment in the element of the air. I wonder anxiously if she will ever learn to fly — there's a major intellectual leap forward needed here.

In the last two days she's developed a major problem with her claws, those needle-sharp talons which have punctured me so often lately. They catch on everything — clothes, her bedding, the carpet when she walks on it — they cause her severe annoyance and she gets in little frets and tantrums, biting at her foot to get the offending threads or fabric off. This morning she managed to hook herself up on the little bit of curtain which was covering her cardboard den in the aviary, sort of hung there, standing on one leg, the other tethered, for I don't know how long before I came back from the dogs' walk at half past nine. She was not in a panic or a frenzy, but definitely wasn't too happy either. For the first time ever she hadn't eaten her breakfast mouse, not would she after she was unstuck. She left it until one o'clock, the equivalent of a Lenten fast for Hesper.

Needless to say, I removed the piece of curtain forthwith.

The aviary experiment has definitely been upsetting and depressing her a little. Some of the bubble has gone out of her.

Decided after the accident this morning, which was not serious but might well have been, that we must cut her claws today, a task I dreaded. The last time we did this was with Buddy, the crow, and he struggled like a mad thing. It is impossible to see where the vein in the claw ends on the crow, the talons being pitch-black, and I accidentally cut into the quick. It bled profusely which made me feel terrible.

Dreaded the same thing happening with Hesper, but as we had to perform the operation we might as well get all the horrors over and done with at once and put on her aylmeri (falconry anklets) at the same time. I checked all my books about eighteen times. We debated whether to wrap Hesper in a towel, as is usual practise, but decided she is so used to being picked up that it would cause her less distress to be restrained in this way. So I held her on her back, with her little feet in the air, and Jon wielded the hawks' clippers. She was as good as gold, seemed very relaxed and occasionally nibbled my hair, though there were one or two indignant little squeaks, not from pain as we definitely didn't hurt her but perhaps from dislike of the tweaking motion. Jon just took the little translucent tips off — they were like those tiny colourless prickles you get stuck in your hand from clearing up brambles in the garden.

Then it was time for the aylmeri. Jon made a cock-up of the first one, by putting the eyelet on the wrong side of the pliers, and riveting together aylmeri, Hesper and pliers for all eternity. He said to Hesper 'You'll have to drag that lot round with you for the rest of your life'. Hesper definitely not amused and began to struggle violently though she soon calmed down again. Then at last Jon got the aylmeri on right, and we put her back in her box. I was astounded by how calmly she had taken it all. After this kind of indignity, Buddy would be a bundle of black staccato exploding neuroticism for days but Hesper as always took everything in her stride and just continued to be her usual philosophical amiable self.

She did not appear to notice the aylmeri at first — possibly with all the tangling up she had been doing to herself for the previous forty-eight hours they were just one more dimly perceived aggravation. Later, however, she got very cross with them, pulling at them savagely with the nearest approach to wildness I have ever seen in her. They are big buff anklets, made of soft leather. I'm not going to put the jesses through them for three or four weeks, but just get her used to wearing them — her young bones are too soft to take any kind of strain yet.

9th June

For the last two days I have been carrying Hesper out to the aviary before breakfast, so that she can spend most of the day in there — I bring her in again about three or four in the afternoon. She travels on the glove very confidently, though you can still feel a slight nervous tremble in her legs and by the time we arrive she is gripping tightly.

When you first put her in the aviary she is very funny: she runs about, doing the hop skip and jump routine, and I can't help dawdling there, watching her. Both yesterday and today I've gone back indoors at ten to eight to find Jon has already started making the breakfast. It is a sacred matrimonial tradition that I am the one who has to make the breakfast — it is a criminal dereliction of duty if I don't. Jon NOT in a good mood, banging about and doing a lot of heavy sighing. Everything's playing him up — the butter knife purposefully jumps out of his hand onto the floor — the toaster plays the bitch and won't go down, then burns the bread and won't pop up again — the microwave clock lies like a heathen and the egg gets overdone. I'm smiling, laughing silently at Hesper's latest cute tricks, how she attacked the sand for example, scratching it, pecking it, then spitting it out. She has started her own self-taught flying lessons again, which consist mainly of putting her two feet together very neatly and springing upwards in the air with wings outstretched, not flapping, so she gets up a couple of inches and then comes down again — in other words, a certain vital ingredient is missing. This morning she has done this for five minutes, and then a lot of bombing about, running, so that I can see I'm going to have to rearrange the furniture, the logs, the artistic dead tree, so that she's got more room for these gyrations. I recount these endearing little nonsenses to Jon. Jon just goes 'Humphh!' with a sour expression like the Kipling camel.

The aylmeri don't seem to disturb her any more, in fact she seems to have forgotten all about them. She doesn't even notice them when she's lying down, or rather sitting on her haunches, her feet stuck out in front of her. She screws her little toes up in a ball; they look very pretty, like little monkeys' paws, the lethal talons curved out of sight. Her feet take on quite a different appearance when she's got something to eat. She picks up a mouse and you can see those wicked talons curl in slowly, mechanically, with a vicelike grip, in an action which would kill a living mouse — barn owls sometimes kill merely by squeezing their prey to death, sometimes by a hammer blow to the base of the skull.

The feet on a bird of prey are what are used for self-defence, not the beak. The bigger raptors can cause the most terrible puncture wounds and lacerations to the human hand, the part of the body which is most often near them. The grappling action, where all the talons turn in and lock tighter and tighter, is called footing — it's excruciatingly painful and very difficult to unlock, as instinctively the talons tighten and penetrate deeper the more the enemy or prey struggles. Alan took great delight in telling me once about a man who had had half his face ripped off by his eagle. Alaska, Alan's Bald Eagle, certainly has the capability to cause the most horrific injuries.

Hesper has never shown any aggression towards me, though occasionally she will use her little nipping beak for reprimand and admonishment. Sometimes she reacts as if she thinks I want her food, want to rob her of her filthy little treasure. Her reaction to this is to chitter in annoyance and warning, and to stomp off tightly into a corner, face turned inwards, wings arched over, and eat the thing in security where I can't get any of it.

11th June

In the afternoon on Friday there was suddenly a definite and dramatic change in her mood. It was almost as if some switch had been flicked, some hormonal trigger or genetic blueprint activated — suddenly she became much more active, quite bossy and headstrong, and began careering round the aviary in a very reckless fashion. She had hardly eaten at all, only chewed the head off her breakfast mouse, and I was half wondering if she was sick, only that was impossible to believe with that energetic, slightly fey performance going on. A fly flew into the aviary through the wires, bumbled about a bit and alighted on one of the logs, and she ran after it, wings sort of clenched up tight round her body and a very determined look in her eye as if to say 'I'm going to get you, you stupid buzzing bastard'. She missed of course. I had things to do, and only came back at six to take her indoors. She seemed much calmer. This was a most misleading impression. Back in the house, in her usual tray, she immediately jumped over the side, onto a newspaper on the counter. I put her back. She then spent the next ten minutes, craning with the greatest curiosity over the edge of the counter, looking down at the cats ranged all three together on the floor eating their supper. I didn't dare leave the room for a moment in case she did something crazy.

She spent the evening getting ever more rampageous and out of control. We were watching a video. About nine Jon had a very long business call to take, and while he was down in the office I decided the only thing to do with the owlian maniac was to put her outside for the night. Took her out, put her in the aviary which didn't seem to please her very much, and went away. As I went back to the house, I could see my breath hanging in the air — it's been a really cold June and the night was almost autumnal. Got in a fret — I can't leave her out here — it's much too cold. Decided after half an hour I would bring her in again, that it was just not a suitable night for her first spent out of doors, on her own, no longer in a centrally heated house. Went back around ten and brought her in. Hesper definitely more subdued now. She had eaten her mouse at last, and was quiet for the rest of the evening.

On Saturday she began again. In the morning she was climbing madly up the wires and trying to escape from her cage. I took her out to the aviary straightaway with her breakfast. After the antics of yesterday, I decided to leave her out there for a long time to burn her energy off. I did not bring her back in until half past seven at night, the longest time she has ever been out.

When I went to fetch her, I was greatly impressed. She was on one of the low stumps and she launched herself off it and glided two feet or more down into the sand, a really impressive breakthrough. The word 'flight' implies something far more strenuous and stressful than her true effortless thistledown buoyancy. I could see I was not going to have to gloomily fantasise any more about her never learning to fly because she couldn't see anybody else doing it.

I stayed watching her, fascinated. Then suddenly the cat slunk up, appearing on the other side of the wire, the scrofulous old Bunny, who stood up on her hind legs to peep over the boards which form a solid barrier at the bottom of the wire. Her little black pointed head, with its white smudge, looked positively satanic and malevolent, the eyes blazing full of murder as she stared at Hesper. Through the wire she hooked her claws, those talons which always infect the slightest scratch they make, and you could see the transparent hooks grappled to the wire. Hesper looked totally unconcerned by this evil apparition, and trotted up to take a closer look. Luckily at this point the cat, unable to take the stress of the unnatural position, fell off. I doubt very much that she could hook the bird through the one-inch galvanised mesh, but it was not a nice sight all the same.

Took Hesper indoors. It was immediately apparent that she was in an even more obstreperous mood than the previous night. At once she jumped out of her tray and proceeded to try to throttle herself, first in the flex of the wall telephone, which could easily have fallen down and bonked her on the head, and then with some plastic trimmings on a cardboard box. It was impossible to leave her in the kitchen on her own. I put her back in the tray, put the cage bars over it, and removed the whole contraption to the sitting room. I hoped that the old fascination of the window would do the trick, that and the company and the noise of the television would calm her restlessness. The old window magic worked for an hour — I watched the telly and soaked up the whisky and prayed for peace. Jon in Cornwall, gone to see his mother for the last time — she is dying of cancer. About nine Hesper started to get very very restless again. She started trying to claw her way out, then to force her little face out though the bars; finally she jumped up, wings flapping, and clung to the side bars, her wings making a ping against the metal. We had evidently come to crisis point, the moment I had been dreading for a fortnight, when the existing arrangements completely fell to bits. It was impossible to leave her loose, alone, anywhere in the house without either a) her killing herself with the most likely or unlikely object, or b) me throttling her for wrecking the place and shitting everywhere. It was impossible to watch the telly with that flapping histrionic racket going on. It was warmer than the previous night, my breath no longer making clouds in the air. I said to myself that there had come a point when the damage she was likely to do herself indoors infinitely outweighed the possible damage outside. I tried one last trick, the old blanket-over-the-cage trick, which used to work so well for Buddy. Hesper patently not Buddy, being a bird of the night, but it was worth a shot. Blanket trick fails deeply and abysmally — Hesper making more racket than ever, running up the bars of the cage, and rattling them infernally. I'm very tired, I'm very frayed, it's been a long day. Suddenly I take the decision I've been fearful of for days, I whip Hesper out of the cage, put her in a box (no pussyfooting about with the glove and training now), go down to the aviary, put her on her log, leave her a mouse, and stomp off without a backward glance.

Back to the sofa, light a fag, drink another tot of whisky, watch the film. Twenty minutes later I'm attacked by a huge black obliterating wave of the guilts. It's too cold out there, too frightening; the night noises will be strange to her; she'll freeze to death in the middle of June. I can't stand the tension and I go to check up on her. I can't see her, because she's gone into her little cardboard refuge, but I can hear her hissing loudly and imperatively. For a moment I dither, feel an agony of indecision. But if it is not tonight, it must be tomorrow, or the day after, or the day after that — sometime she has to be left to her own devices. I look up: the night is mild, there is no chance of rain. I harden my heart, and go away, and leave her.

The natural result of this is that I spend the most appalling night, waking with a start every couple of hours, and dreaming convoluted dreams of Hesper. The last time I wake up it's quarter to six and daylight. I'm wide awake in an instant — should I go out now and save her? I'll have to bring her in, warm her up, as she's bound to be suffering from hypothermia despite roofed-in aviary with three solid walls, and cardboard castle, full of newspapers and rags, carefully positioned well off the floor, out of the way of draughts, in the very warmest corner.

More callous side of personality intervenes, asserting that all this is a lot of fuss about nothing, and she's either okay or dead, in either of which states she can perfectly well stay where she is. Callousness prevails. I go to sleep again, a thick drugged dense sleep, which is shattered with difficulty by the alarm clock at eight o'clock. I immediately go out to check up on her. And naturally the aggravating little sod is perfectly alright. In fact it looks like she's been having an all-night party, as the aviary, which I cleaned up the previous afternoon, is dotted all over the place with tiny patches of white. The midnight feast of a white mouse is gone. In other words ALL IS FINE.

14th June
Problems grow along with enchantment — she is incredible fun, as cute as cute can be, but now she has the ability to fly (airborne to a height of three feet or so), there has come an enormous exponential growth in curiosity. Her former philosophy and calm have evaporated, and instead she's rampaging about (if anything so featherweight can be said to rampage) and sticking her little face into absolutely everything.

We're in the kitchen this afternoon, a very amusing but harassing half hour spent resolutely watching her and steering her away from the dogs' den — where Sasha, disgusted with the inordinate amount of attention this feathered fluffball gets, has turned her back and gone to sleep, and Lushka, consumed with jealousy, keeps a bright eye though the bars of the dog gate and every now and then gives vent to a shrill high yap, of frustration, challenge and aggression.

Hesper has a funny little note you only ever hear when she's exploring. It is very subdued but very sweet, a liquid bubble of sound, rather pensive, with an interrogative pitch to it: 'What's going on here? What's this then?' Her vocal repertoire is one of the most surprising things about her — before she came, I had no idea that owls had so much in the way of vocabulary. When she is at her most amiable, she has a lovely musical twitter, which one is always trying to get out of her because it's so charming to hear. Then there are the hisses, which come in several different shades: the Conversational 'I'm here. You there?' repeated over and over again; the Aggressive, in a more strident tone, 'That's my mouse. Clear orf!'; and the Fractious, usually breaking off into chitters, 'Pack that in, you irritating git', terminated by a crotchety peck of the beak. When she gets really angry, though, it seems she just goes deathly silent, freezes up, all grim, and still, and furious.

15th June
Hesper's very nearly free of the bum fluff now, just a sort of thick fluffy white scarf around her neck and the odd white wisps here and there over her back — they're sort of pendant from the uttermost tips of the adult feathers, hanging there so filmy and so delicate that you can gently pull them off without causing her the slightest twinge.

Over the last five days or so, the most enchanting little sprinkle of iron-grey drops have appeared on her belly and underneath her wings, where the feathers are snow-white. The drops are demi-transparent, as if painted on gauze — they are so delectable that they make a perfect finish to her beauty.

She remains very very fluffy and white around her drawers, which remind me sometimes of Victorian bloomers and at other times of Regency breeches — these, with her lovely golden wings, make her look very richly and charmingly dressed, like some gorgeous apparition from the past. She never looks like anyone in modern clothes — there's just no equivalent in the sort of stuff we wear — the material is not rich enough, and the cut doesn't sufficiently exaggerate the body shape.

Lately I've been putting the jesses on her, more for practise than anything else and to stop her being a nuisance and jumping off the glove when I don't want her to. She is now excellent at sitting on the glove, perfectly adapted to the movement of walking, and making no complaints if I adjust her position slightly because she's sitting in the wrong place. About four or five times she has bated away from the glove, and been pulled up short by the jesses. Each and every time she has of her own accord and with the utmost adroitness turned and flown straight back to the glove. I try hard not to let this happen too often, so as not to strain her legs.

Yesterday for the first time I put on not only the jesses but the swivel and the leash. It was a sunny afternoon for once, and I let her go on the lawn, knowing that she could not as yet muster up the power to fly up into the trees — not that she would do so as a means of escape, being perfectly happy and contented with her lot in life, but because of that restless, bright-eyed, endlessly inquiring curiosity of hers which has become so extreme in recent days. She shows the greatest fascination of all for dank holes and dusty dirty corners, all the worst bits round the house, like the half-bricked-up hole by the steps, or the stony bit under the metal stairs, or any old drain, ugly and insalubrious — these dank pits she positively beams at every time she sees them and she scuttles towards them with every appearance of rapture. She ignores other things you think she would be fascinated by, such as an immense stag-beetle which was wandering around on the lawn near what appeared to be the sawn-up remains of a rival. It was an amazing creature, ebony black, polished and glossy, with antlers a deep arterial red. No wonder they used to call it the devil's coach-horse. Hesper momentarily watched its lumbering and ungainly progress through the blades of grass, but with very little interest and soon went on to something else. She is not indifferent to all insects though, but is immediately rapt with attention for anything that buzzes, large flies or bees in particular — she doesn't appear to differentiate between them.

I had my first scratch from her a couple of days ago, accidental of course. It is very tempting to put her on my shoulder, but also a great mistake as she likes this perch a great deal better than anything else and once she is on it I have little control of the situation. It is difficult to move her with one hand, and her natural response to me trying to move her is to dig her claws in because she feels insecure about her footing. This is painful, but nothing like as painful as when she decides that the next move must be onto my head. Eight needles inserted accupuncturally in the scalp are not an experience I feel called upon to repeat very often. I want her off there as soon as possible, even to the point of getting rough and knocking her off as the less comfortable she feels the more she sticks the needles in. On this particular occasion, somewhere in the resultant mêlée she scratched my hand. It did not get inflamed like one of Bunny's scratches, or the wound delivered to my knee by Hesper's harassed parents — that took a good two or three weeks to go away. From this I must conclude that Hesper's living arrangements must be somewhat more sanitary. Or something else — perhaps she cleans under her fingernails, I dunno.

16th June

In the aviary. A beautiful, in fact a too hot, afternoon.

Hesper is fairly full of beans — she's doing a lot of little aggro tips and runs, killing large handfuls of sand, then she flies over and begins dinging my glass of lemonade with her beak. More practise kills — the sand is being slain right, left and centre. She does a curious trick then, feet forward, clenching another dead yellow handful, she flaps slowly backwards, travelling at least a foot or more at a level height above the ground, dragging the sand so it actually makes gouges.

Something which I don't much care for is that she has developed a new habit of eating her food in the sand, constantly rolling her meal in it and therefore ingesting a lot of the stuff.

This morning she was on the floor, eating out the inside of a chick's carcass, tearing tiny slithers of flesh and organs and bones out and eating them with evident relish. She kept the skin and yellow fluffy exterior intact, carefully scooping out the inside like someone eating a boiled egg. I was intrigued to know what she'd do with the hollow carcass when she had finished.

When she had got all the best bits out, she looked around for a brief moment. I thought 'She is full up and doesn't want any more — will she stash the remains or just drop them and leave them?' Instead Hesper gave a good tug and pulled off one of the legs, swallowing it whole. I thought 'Surely that must be it'. But no, after another, ever more momentary contemplation, she proceeded with great pleasure to swallow the remnants, the last leg attached to the little bag of skin. She then dabbled round frenetically in the sand with her beak, as if searching for any stray morsels she might have dropped She did not *look* for them, she *felt* for them. Then she spat the sandy grains out and scrabbled her beak against the bark of the log, a clumsy gesture, turning her beak once or twice to make sure it was cleaned off properly. She has none of the superb adroitness of Buddy, the crow, who plies his sword-like beak with incredible rapidity and skill, swiftly slashing it from side to side like a chef sharpening a kitchen knife. Hesper's similar motion is ungraceful and probably not very effective.

She uses her beak for nibbling a great deal. It is blunt at the sides, but with a real little needle point at the end. The end hook is used for tearing apart flesh like the chick's. But she can also use her beak with incredible gentleness, either as an exploratory tool, assessing and judging some object close to her, or as a means of caress when she's feeling particularly sweet-natured. When she caresses like this, she always closes her eyelids, the grey nictitating membrane slides right over the eye, whilst the exterior eyelid only comes down to perhaps one third of its extent.

Her eyesight is very questionable close up, in fact she seems to be virtually blind. She can see movement, even right under her nose, but something which is stationery often seems to disappear right into the background for her. Not always though. As yet I haven't quite worked out the apparently contradictory logic behind this short-sightedness.

Barn owls hunt mainly by sound. They can pinpoint a mouse from just two rustling sounds in complete darkness, the first gives the general direction, the second pinpoints the mouse exactly. As they can fly in absolute silence, the prey does not hear them and the sound of their wings does not mask the rustle of the prey if it moves. They are deadly accurate even in pitch black.

Another aid to perfect hearing is the great mobility of the neck — Hesper can with the greatest ease look right down her own back.

There is an old superstition that if you walked round and round an owl, it would going on turning its head to watch you until it eventually strangled itself.

One thing Hesper never objects to is being picked up. She never scolds or nags or shows any annoyance. Now she can fly, she tends to automatically move her wings beneath your enclosing hands — if you then let her wings slip out she flaps merrily until you put her down, but shows no objection to the half-carriage, half-flight arrangement.

Her moods, which are variable, do not seem to correspond exactly with the time of day, though certainly she is generally more active in the evening. Mornings vary a great deal. Yesterday when I went out at about half past eight she was absolutely dozy and soporific, really nodding off on her tree, and looking at me through sleep-drenched eyes, the lids half-closed, like someone who has been up for 36 hours straight. The air of sublime weariness, yet philosophy and calm, which emanated from her was very charming. It must be this consummate appearance of sagacity, of the eternal wisdom of ages, mixed with a look of the most gentle, pleasant and accepting benevolence, which led to the traditional image of the wise old owl, meditative, bolt upright on a branch, with one foot tucked neatly in its undergarments.

> A wise old owl sat in an oak
> The more he saw the less he spoke
> The less he spoke the more he heard
> Why can't we all be like that bird?

20th June

Jon's mother died in the early hours of the night, after a long illness. Sad day, gloom, making plans to go down to Cornwall for the funeral. Holiday cancelled, so no more falconry in Scotland as planned. We're leaving Thursday.

I spend some time with Hesper. The sand in her aviary is still quite damp after all the recent rain, and the wood lice evidently regard it as a sanctuary. One of them bundles across the floor in front of her, and she watches it intrigued, and paddles slowly after it, in no particular hurry and certainly not with the air of one motivated by bloodlust. She arrives at the spot where she marked it, nibbles the floor but finds nothing. The wood louse, evidently more sussed as to the situation than she is, is hurrying off as fast as its many legs can carry it, and has already moved a couple of inches from the original spot. This is yet another example of her rather dodgy eyesight, of how objects close up vanish into a blur for her.

Now her fuzzy glare seems to catch the movement of the fugitive and she moves after the woodlouse again. Woodlouse stops and sagely play dead, and she investigates the sand all round it, even tipping it over once so that it lies with its pale belly uppermost but does not lose its nerve and continues to act the stiff. Hesper fondles and chews the sand with her beak, and eventually the woodlouse gets up and head off for the less unnerving shelter of the log. She sees it again, but again entirely misses catching it. The woodlouse at last makes it to the log, and presses itself up terrified against the bark whilst she, bumbling, investigates all round it in the most desultory and incompetent manner. After a couple of minutes she gives up. The woodlouse lives to fight another day.

After all the dreadful weather of the rest of June, suddenly it's got burning hot. I can't wait for the delivery of the new deluxe hawk bath, and fix up a temporary arrangement instead, thinking Hesper may be glad of a bath.

Young birds of prey do not need water, as they derive all the moisture they need from their food. Later the adults use it for bathing and, very occasionally, for drinks. It will be the first time that Hesper has seen water. Having admired Alan's birds at their daily ablutions, I imagine that she will greet the water with rapture, or at the very least with immense curiosity, but to my huge disappointment she gives it no attention. After much coaxing and persuasion, temptingly splashing the water about and making it sparkle in the sunshine, I manage to get Hesper to look at her bath for all of about thirty seconds before she turns away and gets on with the usual favourite occupation of staring out of the wire of the aviary. I lose patience and pick her up off the log and put her down next to the bath — more play noises — more splish-splash-splosh — cries of 'Come on in, the water's lovely!' — Hesper continues her look of stoical indifference. Now I'm really mad — I pick her up and put her in the water. She appears to hardly notice that a curious chilly substance is lapping round her ankles. She stands there patiently indulging me for a moment and then gets out. Later in the day I repeat the whole charade of enticing her to her bath. Hesper regards my antics with mild amusement but the water barely registers 0.001 on the Richter scale of her consciousness. I go away in a huff.

When I come back a couple of hours later, intending to remove the temporary bath, I find the perverse creature standing in it. She tastes it, taking little head-shaking sips, more like eating than drinking, almost as if she is trying to tear bits off it, and she appears to waffle it round her mouth like a wine connoisseur. She doesn't appear particularly enamoured of it, but it is decided now that the bath will stay.

Dozy she may be, but still she will stand companionably on your knee for hours, much intrigued by the rattle of the pen across the paper, occasionally reaching out to investigate with her beak. Her serenity is profound. Occasionally she performs a little laid-back brushing and combing, and always there continues the intermittent low rasp of her conversation.

She's developing the palest coffee ruff, just under her chin. It is the most delicate colour, café-au-lait, a distinct band against the snowy white of her breast. This coffee ruff and the spots on her breast and the underside of her wings confirm that she is female (though there can be some plumage variations and the diagnosis is not infallible).

26th June
Monday. In Bournemouth, having come to see Jon's father. The funeral was last Friday. We're going home today — an immense relief.

We stayed in St Mawes on Thursday and Friday, then just outside St Austell on the Saturday night. There were buzzards, two or three of them, wheeling stately and slow in the immense sky when we arrived at the hotel, a wonderful sight in their graceful dignified nonchalance. They made hardly any effort at all, simply gliding on the thermals with the merest casual flick of a wing tip to change direction. The best place to see them was in the clearing cut in the woods where there are two practise golf tees. Apparently the buzzards nest in the woods there and filch the occasional bunny rabbit, a welcome theft one would imagine as all the tees are covered with little round rabbit pellets — there is hardly an inch of space clear of them, the fresh ones dark brown and the old ones bleached straw-coloured by the sun.

I asked the owner of the hotel (it was a small place, very pretty, without much in the way of staff, and he was cleaning the terraces outside the house by himself) 'Are those buzzards up there?' 'Yes, we have a lot of them.' 'Are they common buzzards?' He stared at me as if I was deaf or bonkers or both. 'Yes, we have a lot of them.' It took a moment of two to get the conversation back on the straight and narrow, an experience which was repeated several times during our stay.

Once he had comprehended I was asking what sort of buzzard they were, he said that he hadn't known that there was more than one sort. This should have been the end of the matter, but he kept giving me odd, suspicious and amazed glances. These intensified after I asked him if he spent most of his time in the garden, which he interpreted as meaning I took him for the odd-job man —with mild hauteur he informed me 'My wife and I own the place'. 'I know you own the place,' I snapped back, suddenly feeling intensely irritated.

It was rather like conversing with a Venusian. Nothing Jon or I said was ever taken the right way. Lunchtime was another feast of ghastly misunderstandings because, while he was serving us, he persisted in trying to engage us in polite conversation. We had to nod, smirk, ask questions, make remarks of our own, all of which seemed only to make him even more boggle-eyed.

The suspicion that he was indeed from another planet grew every time we ran into him and was completely confirmed during the course of the evening. Now for the first time out of his old gardening rags, togged up in a suit, polished shoes, white shirt and tie, very dapper, he was full of the most amiable social graces and entertained us with talk of his days as an accountant in the City, his high-flying days (Me to Jon: 'If he is a high-flyer, I'm a bacon sandwich'), and even insisted on getting out a photograph of his old team to show us, pointing out superfluously 'Of course, I was much younger then'.

There were five of us having supper in the large dining room which could have taken 25 to 30. The owners were dining companionably with an unfortunate lady guest. Then there was one other couple and us.

The Venusian's wife was an extremely brisk, abrupt, strident, domineering woman with a megaphone of a voice. We heard a lot of stuff about Queen Mary's kleptomania, and how pathetic the current Royal family is. The conversation was more or less public and generally directed at the centre of the room, and every so often the Venusian came over to see how greatly we were enjoying it.

At last, unable to take any more, we skipped the last course and fled to the lounge. Even there we were not safe. The

Venusian followed us, ostensibly to light the fire, but probably to check in his well-meaning but inane way that we were all right. He lay down on the hearthrug in front of the fireplace, literally at our feet, and started rolling about and making conversation like an antiquated and nightmarishly hideous cat. And then his REAL cat walked in. Oh unfortunate cat, a lithe slim ginger-tinted Burmese. It wandered amiably up to its master, who, glad of a bit of moral support, told us all about this cat, about the cat's sister and how she had been run over, and how the pair had been named after his parents ('As a compliment — at least I hope that they took it as a compliment') and how he had had to ring up his mother to tell her that her namesake was dead, which was very embarrassing. He then said that the remaining cat liked games, and before our startled and frankly horrified eyes laid into the cat violently, slapping, smashing and hitting it, rolling it about the carpet with no gentle hand, and in short generally beating the shit out of it. The attack lasted for perhaps 30 seconds and then the cat thankfully escaped, retreating to a safe distance, where it began to wash itself frantically to recover its composure. The Venusian laughed in a carefree manner and said that it was unfortunate that the cat had got away so soon because he usually swung it round by its tail. He then got off the hearthrug at the summons of his imperious lady wife, who wanted him to take some food up to another guest who was wisely keeping to her room. We got the hell out of there before he could come back.

Our room was in the top wing of the house, and as we walked up the outside steps towards it we could see a dark long-tailed shape roosting in the tall trees beside our sitting room. All night long the peacock's voice sounded, a very primaeval call, strangely reminiscent of dinosaurs and steaming swamps. I saw the bird itself the next morning, preening itself by a garden bench, with a tumble of gorgeous discarded feathers around it, some of which I picked up. The peacock did not appear to like me staring at it, and after a while stalked somewhat waspishly and effeminately off, carrying its immense weight of tail.

We left the hotel about eleven. There were buzzards for miles of country afterwards — it was evidently a brilliant region for them. One glided over the road many feet overhead, directly above the car, and as I looked up I could see the sun shining through its pinions and the distinct white slashes on the undersides of its wings. A few miles further on I got another close view of one, sitting on a fence post as we flashed past — I could just make out the slightly raggedy white vicar's collar which it wore, set off by its rusty brown feathers.

There was a great pleasure in looking out for the buzzards and the sky seemed empty and sad when they finally disappeared.

We met Jon's father that afternoon, and went to Merley Bird Park for an hour. There was a captive buzzard there. It was calm and peaceful and appeared contented with its lot in life as it sat on its perch in a spacious aviary. It had amazing yellow lipstick that ran back from its beak along the rims of its mouth. A handsome kindly looking bird. Now it glanced upwards into the sky, perhaps spotting some passing bird of prey, even one of its own kind, immensely high up, and it let out a mournful melancholy cry, exactly the same cry we had heard echoing in the skies at St Austell, a eerie stirring otherworldly sound which sent a shiver down my back.

Also saw at Merley another peacock, this time in full amorous display. He put forth all his charms for his lady love, bringing up his tail to the erect fan shape, and then tilting it a little further forward, so it made a sort of bower for his body and his head. Then, very stiffly and slowly, he shifted from side to side, to show his glory off from all best possible angles. His backside, however, he kept well away from her, which was just as well as it was less than enchanting. There was nothing left to cover it up, and all you could see was a plain brown bum like a chicken's with a lot of long naked white quills splaying out of it.

The female was unimpressed by his efforts and disappeared under a low bush where he couldn't possibly follow her. Gradually his tumescence subsided, the tail flattening slowly back — he then spent the next few minutes irritably rearranging it, rattling the quills together with a peevish, hurried, ill-tempered movement, as if he was raking an enormous pile of hay.

In other aviaries there were various owls, a tawny owl, a little owl, two barn owls, all hiding well back in their enclosures. More conspicuous were the two Bengals, sitting together on a branch. The prettiest one had the most delicious colouring, all delicate pearls, mushrooms and ash-greys, with dark smoked markings, speckles and bars. Both perched bolt upright, with a very military posture, which belied their sleepy blinking eyes and a general air of something somnolent and feline — there was a distinct whiff of the cat about them.

In the next aviary to them, a very big one, there were the european eagle owls, the largest owls in the world, immense ungainly clumsy-looking birds with legs and claws enclosed in thick golden-beige felt. If the Bengals were catlike, these were ursine, with their great fluffy teddy-bear bodies, large heads, no-necks, and furry stumpy legs. Their eyes, however, are unutterably magnificent. I remember at Alan's when his eagle owl, which was kept in the aviary at the back, came down with a thump on the little platform behind the foodhatch and my first sight of it was nothing but eyes, the whole space of the hatch being filled with those blazing round rose-gold headlamps.

The two eagle owls at Merley seemed somewhat lethargic in the heat, but eventually one of them stomped over to the foodtray, only partially shaded from the blazing sun, where ten or twelve large week-old chicks lay limp, yellow and dead. The owl selected one and walked off with a portly gait like a fat alderman. Some boys passed, saw the chicks, and went 'Yuck, that's cruel' — usual reaction — bet they're not vegetarians. Stood watching the owl dilly and dally about whether it was going to eat its meal or not, and as I did so I smelt that familiar charnel-house odour of an aviary which isn't cleaned out often enough, though in my limited experience it is less the mutes that count (for any offensiveness in them goes off very quickly) and more the remains of dropped chick yolk and rotten meat, a distinctive pong which hints of rifled graveyards.

2nd July

We will have been back home a week tomorrow. After all the really tumultuous and disturbing events of Jon's mother's death and funeral, and other upsetting family affairs, I've found it very difficult to get back into the old rapport with Hesper. She's so moth-like, so delicate, so unassertive, so pale, soft and glimmering like a moonbeam, that it is difficult for me to reassert her former pre-eminence against the lurid and deafening tumult of human affairs. Her gentleness, her philosophical nature, her perfect amiable acceptance of my appearances and disappearances, don't provide a dramatic enough counterbalance.

Realising that something has got to be done if she is not just to become a vague presence at the bottom of the garden, ever since we got back I've been bringing her out for at least an hour a day in aylmeri, jesses and leash, and tying her to her bow perch to get her used to being tethered. She's done pretty well at it. She's never left alone in case the dogs or cats attack her — she continues utterly fearless of them and treats them just like another set of owls. A couple of days ago Sasha put her face up to sniff her and received a peck with that sharp little beak right in the middle of her shiny black nose. Startled and outraged, the immense dog jumped back from the minute puff of bird — one weighs six or seven stone, the other ten ounces, but there's no doubt that on this occasion the featherweight came off the victor.

Hesper can't be let free on her own, as I was doing even up to the time we went away. For one thing, I've no idea exactly how high she can fly. Before it was always a limit of about six feet — now I suspect from the way she eyes up and judges various attractive perches, that it is more likely twelve feet or more. Once up in the branches of the trees, she would never come back until she was starving, for she would just go higher and higher exploring the strange new world about her.

On Friday Rick came over. He was amazed by her prettiness, really enchanted and mesmerised by it, but at the same time she obviously made him slightly nervous. It was the usual scenario, a group of chairs in the garden, Hesper ostensibly tethered to her bow perch but in reality moving from chair-arm to table to grass to flagstones to flowerpot and back again. Rick kept his distance, though he continued to admire her. Then Jon came out and I fetched the sandwiches for lunch. Rick took a thick one, sausage, bacon and egg, took a bite out of it, laid it on his plate, laid the plate on the table, and the next moment Hesper flew down on top of the sandwich, with that particular smug look she has when she's judged a complicated angle to a nicety. Her little feet, with their immensely long toes and talons, curved appreciatively over the peculiar cushion. Jon and I of course burst out laughing. Rick indignant — 'I'm not eating that now'. I picked Hesper up — luckily she did not attempt to fasten her claws in the sandwich. Rick moodily picked the top slice off and gave it to the dogs.

The hot weather had definitely put Hesper off her own food, so that she is eating about half as much as before. To my great annoyance, as always when she is toying with her meal, she daubs and rolls it in the sand as if she is covering it with breadcrumbs. If she then abandons it, I'll only spot it next time I go to see her because of the great fat hairy bluebottles buzzing round it. Also there are often five or six ants running in circles round the coated remains. I always chuck these pieces out for the crows and bring her fresh supplies.

A further annoyance, she will insist on eating her meals in the space immediately behind the door. A couple of days ago she had evidently returned to her flyblown leavings just as I came to see her, and when I opened the door I sent her rolling over and over, one somersault after another, for being so light and airy she could not stop herself. This made her unutterably furious, but for me it was extremely funny seeing an owl turning cartwheels.

Though the weather has been blazingly hot, she does not appear to use her waterbowl to cool down but just takes little revolted sips out of it. Today as I was taking her indoors, we got caught in a passing shower. It was light rain and she delighted in it, holding out her beautiful wings, taut and arched, and spreading out her little tail, so as to make the maximum surface to catch the rain. After that she groomed herself with evident enjoyment and pleasure.

7th July
The new expensive hawk bath has arrived, as replacement for the plastic dogbowl which has been doing duty so far. The only problem is that the thing is IMMENSE — it is eagle- or possibly Roc-sized — she needs a swimming costume, goggles and waterwings to get across it. It will have to stay outside, as it would be impossible to get it in and out of the aviary without all the water sloshing on the floor. In fact it's going to be pretty useless altogether. The great broad rim is too slippery for her tiny feet. She has flown down on the edge and slithered in, twice, which has made her very cross. Though the weather is still baking hot, the water holds nil attraction for her and she does none of that enchanting ducking and fluttering and chucking water over her back that Owly used to do at Alan's. Indeed she gets out of the bloody thing as quickly as possible.

She's in a very fidgety mood this afternoon, up and down from the chair-arm to the grass all the time, and twanging and biting her jesses in the intervals. 'No! If you do that you'll have to go back in the aviary.' And then she desists and begins to preen instead, before once more petulantly pulling at the straps.

She looks particularly pretty in the bright sunshine. Her feet, set in star shape on the chair arm, are a greyish-brown on top with fine white edgings to the scales and a light dusting of white hairs, delicate as those on a woman's arm. Underneath, her feet are a sort of musky coral-brown, and they have the most curious pads on them, three quite separate ones under each toe, coloured a sort of musky yellow. Her talons are iron-grey and at least an inch long. When in the aviary , nine times out of ten she stands on one leg with her other foot bunched up in the soft feathers of her breast. Sometimes the foot is so perfectly concealed in the soft plumey white that the effect can be very startling when it very slowly and thoughtfully emerges, still contracted in a sort of iron fist, the talons of which open and close as if with the languid pulse of her thoughts.

That strange little perfume she had when she was a baby, that hint of old abandoned churches and tombs, she has lost that perfume completely. Now she just smells agreeably dry and warm, a comforting pleasant unassertive smell, like a good book.

The squirrels are back on the lawn again, eating the birds' food. They court death every day, eating within a foot of the crouching cats. Yesterday there were three of them, ranged in a semicircle inches away from the Mother Cat. Also present were the crow family, baiting the cat by walking round three inches behind her tail. We have undoubtedly helped to bring up this fine raucous family of four, whose parents pick up the scraps every day. The youngsters are great fat glossy things, twice the size of their mother and father. Though full grown, they still have lurid vermillion insides to their mouths and megaphone-style voices which shriek for attention — the harassed parents, picking up their own food off the lawn, occasionally stuff a beakful down these gaping holes to shut them up, which leads to a horrible gargling asphyxiated cry as the young crow is cut off in mid-bawl.

It was raining last Monday morning, and when I went out to feed Hesper and Buddy around 10 o'clock I found a wood pigeon in a catatonic state near the pool. It was so zombiefied that it didn't move an inch as I walked up to it. I caught it and looked it over — it appeared to have little wrong with it apart from the fact that, in a malicious freak, one of the cats had torn out half its tail and the centre feathers of both wings. I put it in the aviary with Buddy, who regarded it with amazed surprise and distaste.

By lunchtime, now dubbed Harold Wilson, the pigeon was waddling around, considerably perked up, and for the next five days it ate like a horse and shat accordingly, great encrusted piles of the stuff quite unlike Buddy's wet, wet, wet consistency. They shared the space on mildly hostile yet tolerant terms, only getting in a muck sweat with one another when both simultaneously trying to escape from my horrific attempts to torture them by bringing them fresh food and water. It is massively unrewarding looking after wild birds, as they never cease treating you as some sinew-cracking, bone-crushing, blood-drinking maniac. I've had Buddy for nineteen months, and he's hardly a bit tamer than when he came, though at least he does me the courtesy of recognising me and throws slightly less explosive neurotic fits with me than with other people.

Now however Buddy has escaped, and it was completely my own fault. The aviary was getting distinctly unsavoury, but cleaning it seemed out of the question with its two demented occupants showing every inclination to dash themselves to smithereens every time I went near them — they would tussle over who would get up the escape route (tree branch) first, Buddy attempting to skewer Harold Wilson with his beak and HW putting on the most stupendous explosive display of flapping which effectively drove Buddy off — this is apparently the best defence in the pigeon's armoury and probably accounts for the cat abandoning it half-plucked, all that hysterical noise and commotion getting on irritable feline nerves.

By the end of the week HW evidently enormously improved and capable of looking after himself once more. I had no particular desire to keep him — close up, pigeons have an especially inane, stupid and revolting-looking eye, a sort of cretinous black dot surrounded by a circle of pale yellow-white *exactly* the same colour as pus, so the thing looks as if it has a couple of suppurating boils in its head. I decided HW was going to have to fend for himself and released him in the garden — he waddled stupidly about for a while, then remembered his powers of flight, flew up on the fence, then into the yew tree and was soon gone.

However, in getting him out of the aviary I stupidly left the door open for a moment. Never in all the time I had him had Buddy gone anywhere near the door — my proximity always froze him to the spot — he would never take the risk of attempting to get past me. But that frenzied and inane flapping of the pigeon's sent Buddy mad and as I left the aviary he scurried out and away to freedom, bundling over the grass with astonishing speed for his crippled state.

He'll probably be caught by some predator and eaten within a couple of days.

I remember the day I got him. I had seen him for two or three weeks in the fields, but he always bumbled away before I could get anywhere near him. Then one day a Gordon setter knocked him down when he had unwisely strayed too far into the middle of the field. He was feeding with the other crows at the time, and with no hedges or trees nearby he had no chance of escape. As the Gordon setter pounced and knocked him down, all his inky-black friends rose up into the air, making the most prodigious accusatory din, shrieking 'Murderer! Murderer! Murderer!' at the tops of their voices. The racket was so extraordinary that I went out to have a look. I found the girl, who had got hold of the Gordon setter by now, standing ineffectually over the bird. He was paralysed with fright, and just lay there in the frosty grass, his round black bright eye fixed on me, intent, terrified, and yet unwilling to lose the dreadful sight of his killer approaching, about to shut out the beloved light forever. I picked him up, and still he would not look away from me, though his beak gaped wide with fright. He had the prettiest bluish sheen to his black feathers. I have always loved crows, so I took him home with me.

Buddy lived in the kitchen until I got the aviaries built. He hardly ever groomed himself, but when he did he would ruffle out his feathers with a sploshing crackling sound exactly like someone shaking out a wet umbrella. He had a passion for scraps, the shells from boiled eggs, bits of cheese, the fat of steak, but his biggest mania was for the small curved bones from rack of lamb — he would go absolutely berserk for these. If we were eating the meal, he would start sharpening his bill in speculation, and keep jumping down from his perch and up again, a rhythmic rattle and thud which went on and on until the end he got what he wanted.

He never got tame but he got to know some of our ways. With him one could never cross that gap between a wild bird and the predators who have persecuted his race for centuries. Brenda said to me about Buddy 'Well, he must like *you.*'

'No, he doesn't.'

'Why not, when you look after him so well?'

'Suppose you were in captivity, kept behind bars, tenderly looked after by colossal tigers — would you ever trust them?'

'No.'

Despite his mixed diet, Buddy got scruffier and scruffier. He was always on edge, fanatically nervous. He got painfully thin. He was never happy. So perhaps it is better that some weasel or fox gets him now than he goes on for years and years in a captivity he hates.

8th July

This tough no-nonsense attitude soon wore off, and I started searching the garden for the idiot bird. Located him in a tree, a tall slender sloping hazel, which like all the trees along the brook is so starved of light that it grows at a slant towards the nearest patch of sky. He was about ten feet up. He looked quite a pretty sight, framed against the leaves, the twilight sky behind, and none of the scrawny rents in his black apparel showing in the green-shaded gloaming. He shuffled on the branch, and appeared relieved and joyful to be out in the great wide world again. As I was in no mood to start climbing trees (I was on my own, it was nine o'clock at night, and I had had a couple of whiskies) I left him to it, thinking he'd be okay, he'd manage.

And indeed he was still there the next morning, had obviously stayed in the same place all night as the pebbles were white with splashes beneath him. The dismal creature looked at me, and had one of his perennial attacks of the vapours — though all I was doing was looking at him, not even moving, he decided he had to get away from me and began to move higher and higher onto flimsier and flimsier branches. Eventually, quite deliberately, he launched himself into space, a move of such cretinous stupidity that more than ever I doubted the reputation crows have for intelligence. He tumbled to earth in an ungainly, flapping, dog-eared heap, on the wrong side of our fence, on the high bank above the stream. After much trouble and difficulty I managed to startle him back over the fence again; it was very low at that point where the dogs had squashed the wire down. As soon he went over, I ran back into the garden to the spot in the undergrowth where I had seen him disappear. But there was absolutely no sign of him. He was moronic enough to jump out of a tree just because I was looking at him, but now a deep canniness apparently had taken over and no matter how much noise I made, deliberately clumping about and swishing the branches, he had no more convenient *crises de nerfs*.

He kept to cover perfectly. After a while I gave it up as a bad job. At least he was in the garden, where there was food and some protection available so long as he managed to dodge the cats. I went back indoors.

Later I found him standing on the backdoor steps. It was the most extraordinary thing for him to do, to come forty feet across the garden, all out in the open, without any cover at all, and climb the eight steps to the back door. The memory of his months spent in the kitchen must have prompted him. I was so surprised that, instead of going out the front and sneaking round to trap him, I stupidly opened the back door. Of course he went off again, bundling and careering away about 90 miles an hour, his black garments flapping and crackling about him and his crippled gait eating up the ground. He dived into the bushes near the cats' rickety old basking place, a table in terminal decline from rot and woodworm. And that is the last I've seen of him, though Eddie apparently spotted him when we were out shopping.

9th July

Saw nothing of Buddy yesterday afternoon. But when Jon was making supper I heard his characteristic voice, the alarm/warning note they all make, each crow with its own individual timbre. Went out and located him at the top of the compost heap at the end of the garden by the bridge — Bunny was staring at him, which was what he was protesting about.

I went and asked Jon to help. He insisted on getting out the swimming pool net, a massive unwieldy thing, with which he would have had as much luck in swatting Buddy as the bird shot past him in a streak of tatty black lightening as he would of bagging a bull elephant.

The plan was that I was to run down the footpath and approach from the stream and startle Buddy into Jon's way. Plan went to order, only Jon completely failed to spot Buddy's exodus from the compost heap, saw a flapping, heard a crackling, and then nothing. We couldn't find the bloody bird anywhere. He had completely faded into the background and was invisible. The garden is incredibly overgrown in this corner and there was a multitude of places to hide. Meanwhile the dinner was burning. We went back indoors. Three more times that evening I tried to get him, when I looked out and saw him on the lawn. The last time I saw him he was near the hole in the fence at the front, and I backed off so as not to drive him out into the lane. But there have been no more sightings since that night. The garden feels empty, it feels like he's gone. The cats can't have got him, because there would be a corpse lying around. No explosions of black feathers on the lawn, as if the bird had detonated from the inside, though there is a pigeon disaster area at the top, so perhaps Harold Wilson copped it for real this time.

I feel a bit sad for the idiot bird.

Old Adam, the carrion crow,
The old crow of Cairo;
He sat in the shower, and let it flow
Under his tail and over his crest;
And through every feather
Leaked the wet weather;
And the bough swung under his nest;
For his beak it was heavy with marrow.
Is that the wind dying? O no;
It's only two devils that blow
Through a murderer's bones, to and fro,
In the ghosts' moonshine. *Thomas Lovell Beddoes*

CHAPTER FOUR - DISASTER

19th July
I've been weighing Hesper every day for five days. She steps onto the perch of the weighing machine very obligingly and stands on one foot with benign patience while I fiddle with the weights. Training is going to commence in earnest, which means sharpening up her appetite.

Alan said to starve her for two days, to aim for no more than a 20% drop in body weight, 25% absolute tops. This makes me highly nervous. I'm going to drop her as little as possible.

20th July
Hesper $10^1/2$ ounces this morning. Last night was the first attempt to get her to come to the glove for food. Very poor response. I haven't waited for the two days Alan specified, but chickened out after cutting only two meals.

She should have been ravenous. I had some bits of excellent steak, carefully chopped up for her, but she just looked at them with absolutely no interest at all. She was clearly very hungry, so I finally coaxed her to at least eat out of my fingers and even take one or two steps towards her meal. I thought 'This is going to be a very, very long haul'. My own fault for not starting sooner with her daily food, making her come to get it instead of always dumping it down for her, the policy I adopted when she was tiny to stop that perpetual aggravating hissing.

This morning when I went to see her I was greeted with a very loud and anxious racket. I had brought steak with me again, laced with vitamins. Hesper evidently starving hungry but she had not the slightest intention of eating this unsavoury concoction, just turned it over in her beak and dropped it in the sand. She did this five times in a row, to all four bits of steak, and by that time they looked like nothing on earth. Hesper getting more and more anxious: 'Ain't I going to get no proper breakfast today?' I couldn't stand it. I went and got a mouse out of the fridge and chopped it up. Sat down on her food log with the bits. Brilliant success. Hesper came down to me and then up to the main log again, claimed all four pieces, the largest one last as a reward. Bright-eyed clever little thing.

21st July

Hesper $10^1/4$ ounces this morning.

Having had a miracle breakthrough yesterday morning, I tried again yesterday evening. She was hungry but it was all 'Bring it over 'ere then!' — she would not budge. After ten minutes of fruitless coaxing I gave up, especially as she had now tucked up one foot and gave every appearance of settling down for a bit of philosophising and 40 winks.

Today has been even worse. I'm tired, stressed out and irritable, not at all in the right frame of mind for training. Progress is virtually nil. Hesper getting frantic for food but will not *look*, desperate hissing but she peers absolutely everywhere else than at me; she seems incapable of recognising the food between my fingers. The whole thing is very painful and discomforting in the extreme — I completely lack confidence that this is the right thing to do with my sweet-natured, dozy, little, pea-brained beauty. Meanwhile the dismembered mouse STINKS and drops blood all over the pretty pale suede of the glove. Hesper frantic, upset, ignores me even when I yell, gesticulate, snap my fingers, dangle the bloody object in front of her. When I put it right up close, she only sees it for a moment, will take two or three steps after it, then if I move a little further she just gives up completely. Once or twice she seems almost to have been on the verge of hopping onto the glove, but then has started staring everywhere else again. It's utterly infuriating and upsets both her and me.

22nd July

Hesper 10 ounces this morning.

She's so desperate for food she's hunting in the corners of the aviary for any little odd scraps she might have overlooked.

10 ounces, a big weight loss, 3/4 of an ounce altogether. I'm not at all anxious to go on.

In the evening I'm so mortally pissed off with the whole thing — her anxiety, her misery, my feeling of horrible unease — that I just get her to walk up to the glove and take a whole mouse off it. I can't have all this tormenting, this fretting, and I can't bear the sound of my own voice yelling at her 'Hesp! Hesp! Hesp!' over and over again, ad nauseam.

23rd July

Hesper 10 1/8 ounces this morning.

Just as I was about to completely give up she jumped eight inches for another whole mouse. It seems she'll do it for the whole thing, the shape she recognises, but not for the disparate dismembered lumps

28th July

Hesper has been varying between 10 and 10 1/4 all week.

After the agonies of the previous few days, I decided last Sunday that I would just let Hesper get used to coming for all her meals off the glove. I call her, and utter a 'Key-Yippp!' cry, kind of Pastoral-Arcadian-Shepherd with a touch of Husky-Drover. Some days I have to go 'Key-Yippp!' until my throat is sore. Damned owl looks at everything except at me. The conversation between us gets more and more desperate. 'Do you want the frigging thing or not?' Hesper hisses back madly 'Give it to me RIGHT NOW.' But on other days it works like a dream, and gradually she learns to jump three or four feet.

At that point, thinking all solved, I go back to trying to lure her with small pieces and the thing degenerates into a nightmare again. I hate the decapitated heads, the oozing innards, the chicks dripping and leaking all over me, the intestines from some unfortunate rodent ending up dangling from the glove. One ends up festooned with the stuff, draped all over with it like a serial killer's Christmas Tree.

Picking up the bloody pieces and slapping them on the glove is not even the worse part of it. Hesper frequently completely ignores my solicitations and gazes round steadfastly at the entire surrounding landscape, the galaxy, the universe, in fact everything except the revolting treats which I am so desperate to get rid of. I have to keep on temptingly rearranging things. If she still won't come to me, I have to put everything back in the food container and, peeved and furious, cart it back into the house. In this boiling hot weather everything gets bruised and soggy really quickly. These are the joys of training birds of prey which they never tell you about in falconry books.

Well, that's it. I'm out of here. Maybe I'll try again next year, when I've solved the problems of squeamishness, or even more important moved house, or convinced myself that it's safe to fly Hesper loose round here, with the railway line and the big roads so close. This has been in the back of my mind all along, a horrible black fear of losing her. She is so endearing that I can't bear to take the risk, and with her habitual curiosity and complete lack of fear she would be in mortal danger all the time. I meant to fly her in the fields at the back of us, but every time a strange dog came along I would be going crazy. I would have to get up each morning at five or six and go out before anyone else was stirring. Thus my new interest in owls, which was supposed to be non-stressful, a break from work and all the other human claptrap cluttering up my life, ends up being just another burden. That's it. I'm not flying Hesper. Period.

4th August

The blistering weather at the end of July brought a severe thunderstorm, probably the best daylight thunderstorm I've ever seen. Thunder and lightening well in advance of the storm, building up for at least half an hour beforehand. Gradually the sky went a peculiarly ominous metallic grey, but still the rain held off.

I went out to see how Hesper was taking it. By now the thunder was completely seamless, just one long unbroken shiversome rumble of sound, rolling round and round the heavens and never stopping for an instant. The sky was lit up by two kinds of lightening, a constant flashing and sparkling amongst the clouds, and great long jagged forks crackling down, lighting up the garden with pink phosphorescence. Hesper not at all bothered, gazing out at it all, very interested but not afraid. She would twitter back as I talked, our old delightful fairytale companionship.

Then came torrential rain, like a monsoon — I was stranded at the observation post, and me and Hesp and the aviary nearly floated away.

A day or two later, another truly amazing sight in the garden. The collared doves have been coming down for the bird seed on the lawn, three of them to start with, which dwindled to two, and then one, though I can't be entirely sure of the cause of that. On this particular morning I looked out of the bathroom window and saw the solitary dove alone on the grass. The next instant, this shape in a rush of wind (and almost with a tail of fire like some Old Testament avenger) came hurtling down within millimetres of the dove. The dove shot off at a tangent into the bushes by the stream, escaping murder by a whisker. Its attacker wheeled round and returned so quickly into the hazel tree opposite the bathroom window that still I couldn't make out what it was. But it was definitely still in there — I could hear the rattle of the branches. I waited, and then suddenly this wicked menacing inconceivably evil little head peeped out, surreptitiously, with an insane glare in its eyes, as if hoping that the dove would be idiot enough to come back. It hesitated just for a moment and then shot off across the garden, and I saw its breast was brown with dark brown stripes. It was very large, so large in fact I would have thought it was a goshawk if it hadn't been so obviously brown not grey. It was a female sparrowhawk, the first one I have seen.

The female is the favoured sex in the world of birds of prey. Female sparrowhawks are two or three times larger than their mates. Sometimes they catch and eat them with great relish. The males are about the same size as the prey species, so that what the girls see is not a fellow hawk, a conspecific, but instead a very attractively furnished flying lunchplate.

There have been a pair of tawnies round here almost every night for the last month. You can hear their wondrous stereophonic hooting — one in one tree, one in another some distance away, calling to each other across the gap: 'Whit!' 'To-Whit!' 'Whit!' 'To-Whit!' — very charming, it never palls, even though it goes on for hours and hours without pause or change.

I was very lucky to see them a few days ago, because it is so densely wooded here that though one can hear them perfectly they are too canny to show themselves. I had gone into my bedroom to get something and, hearing the owls, looked out of the window at the twilight sky. The trees on the embankment looked immensely tall and black, and opposite them were the massive oaks of next door's garden. There was just a V shape of sky between the two sets of trees, a dusky golden red with a few delicately tinted clouds. Suddenly a tawny owl left the trees on the embankment and glided across this beautiful, softly and dramatically lit space. It was dark black against the light, with its heavy wedge-shaped form and beautiful powerful rounded wings, the main feathers as clearly distinguishable as fingers. It went down in one lovely effortless curve, not flapping, just gliding and directing its course by minuscule tilts and turns of its wings. It joined its mate and the two of them were just visible in the top of the oaks. After a while they disappeared amongst the leaves though they kept calling to one another for at least an hour afterwards.

The tawnies rattle Hesper, who gets considerably disturbed by their proximity and runs madly up the wire at the front of her aviary, flapping her wings to keep her balance, her white belly and wings ghostly in the darkness. In the morning little bits of her softest down adhere to the wire here and there.

I've decided to get a tawny owl. There's a hand-reared one, ten weeks old, available at Ramsgate.

8th August

I was going to leave at quarter to eight on Saturday morning, to go and collect the tawny owl. Very sleepless night from excitement — broken bits of dreams — once I dreamt that the sparrowhawk had come right up to the windowsill outside my bedroom and was eating its prey there — I distinctly heard a bird scream — in rage or terror, whether a real or an imaginary scream, I'll never know now.

Got up at five to seven, went to get a mouse for Hesper, and walked down to the aviary. She was standing high on her usual perch at the top of the tree. Her facial disks were collapsed in, as they always are when she is sleepy and tired, but such a face with it, frowsy in the extreme — I laughed 'Oh dear, Hesper!', as she looked like someone who had very much got out of the wrong side of bed that morning.

This was all from the front of the aviary before I went in — I had briefly paused to look through the wire before going to unlock the door. As I laughed at her, it struck me with a sudden horrid chill how totally silent she was. She always greets me, either with the little musical burble or the low conversational hiss, a bit more imperative if she is hungry. She was as still as a stone that morning, the most ominous and dreadful stillness, without a sound coming from her.

In a fraction of a second I noticed other things — how that expression on her face was far too extreme to be just sleepiness, how hunched and shocked she was, how the feathers on her left wing appeared to be chipped and broken off, as if somehow she had crashed and hurt herself. I knew now that something was wrong — all this flashing though my mind in an instant — I thought 'Has she broken or twisted her wing?' because it hung down so oddly.

Then I realised that something far more terrible had happened. The feathers were not broken, their tips snapped off — it was that the pure white underside of them had been darkened out against the background of the aviary by the thick blood oozing from her body. I ran round, unlocked the door, went in. She did not move. She was silent, stiff, almost catatonic with shock. Beneath her, gradually soaking into the white sand, was a pool of thick fresh blood.

There was something odd about the way she was standing, the classic barn owl pose, on one leg, the other claw tucked away in the soft feathers of her breast. Only there was an infinitesimal difference. I could not quite define it but something had changed, something had altered in her characteristic shape.

It seemed that her left leg had gone.

This thought seemed so ridiculous, so utterly stupid and bizarre, that I could not take it seriously. I went to lift up her wing, as gently as possible, to see what she had really done to hurt herself, talking to her all the while, but never getting back that sweet little rasp of response. Underneath the wing she was soaked in blood, a bright vital red, with thicker gobbets hanging down, mingled with bits of torn flesh. A huge wound in her side. Unbelievable. Impossible. She had no leg there. I just could not believe it. There was no severed limb to be seen, no sign of any accident, nothing but this terrible injury with no explanation at all of how it had happened.

I fetched Jon. We lifted her down as gently as possible. I was so shocked I was just going to carry her outside as she was, into the garden, on the cardboard tray out of her little box, but Jon said in startled warning 'She can still fly!' and of course she could — I was just not thinking straight. It appalled me to think how nearly I had taken that insane risk. She might have flown into a tree, out of reach — meanwhile all the measures which could have been taken to save her life would not be taken and she would die.

I put her in a box, we went back to the house, rang the emergency number for the local vets. It was a pager number and I left a message. The vet rang back almost immediately. There was only one bird specialist in the practise, and this was not him, nor did he know if the avian vet would be in for surgery that morning. It was the weekend, and all he could say was come into the surgery at nine o'clock and wait to be seen. He was so cool and matter of fact that it began to penetrate for the first time that a bird losing its leg is not at all comparable to the same injury in a human. The vet said in his laconic voice 'Usually there is little blood. Just put her in a box, keep her warm, give her a hotwater bottle, cover her up with a blanket and give her plenty of water to drink.' Then he rang off.

I was not at all happy. Okay, so she wasn't gushing arterial blood, but I wanted her seen as quickly as possible. The vet's attitude was far too laid back to please me. I rang Alan Jones in Crawley, and he said 'I can give you an appointment at quarter to ten'. It was an hour's drive. We had an hour to wait. That was a very very long wait. Hesper had her eyes closed, looked terrible, her little head bowed, blood dripping slowly and wetly from her side.

All I can think is that she's in such a state of shock she's going to die.

The drive takes forever. Even though Jon drives as carefully as possible, she's still banging against the sides of the box all the time. We get to Crawley exactly at quarter to ten. Alan Jones takes her out of the box and lays her on her side on the table. Hesper's bright eye, startled and vaguely alarmed, looks up at us but she doesn't struggle at all, and he examines the wound in her side, ragged bits of muscle and sinew, her living flesh. He touches it gently to show where it needs tidying up. I can't stand this, it's so horrible.

She must have an operation to tidy it up, and he will keep her afterwards, make sure that she recovers from the anaesthetic. I ask, in a steady voice which I absolutely do not feel I possess, 'What are her chances of getting over it?' 'Good.' He says she will adapt remarkably well to life with one leg.

One leg. Oh my beautiful little aerial sprite, my little beauty, the joy of my eyes. She looks so pitiful and pathetic now, bowed over, head falling, eyes closed. I want to say to him 'Please do the best you can for her' — but I can't do it — I can't speak the words. I just mumble something else about how pitiful she looks. 'Yes, she does — *at the moment*'. A rapid glance at me — I am sure he knows what I really meant to say, and in the same oblique way he has given reassurance.

We drive home. All the way I am thinking what a dreadful dreadful shame it is, of all the charming little pretty ways she has, all those endearing little tricks gone forever — the wonderfully comical way that she walks, or rather runs, a sort of bustling self-important little flurry; the way she scratches her head with one elegantly extended claw; the delicious way she pounces, both feet extended; the ritual slow stretch, first one leg and wing, then the other; and best of all that lovely barn owl pose, standing on one foot, the other placed in the soft white down of her breast. All have given me such pleasure to see, time and again. I am devastated for the loss of her beauty.

It was just very bad luck. Almost certainly a weasel or stoat, the vet said, who had passed by and, seeing the owl, had stopped outside, until the owl in her curiosity had gone down the wire to examine it. Then the murderer had grabbed her foot through the wire, would not let go of it however much she flapped her wings and screamed in rage and pain, the creature pulling, trying to drag her bodily through the wire, she pulling to get away, her sinews and hip joint parting under the strain. The pain and terror she went through are terrible to imagine.

Alan Jones has seen two other owls like this in seven years, but apparently parrots being wire-climbers are much more susceptible, and there are seven to eight similar cases a year.

I can't think why none of this has ever been mentioned in any of my books, or by the aviary-building specialists we employed — I went into the matter with immense care, took the specifications of the experts, and this is what has happened — it seems grotesquely unfair.

And yes, I remember now, that the cat hooked itself on the front of the aviary once, and then fell off, but I never thought of the dangers from other quarters, the agile and truly voracious little killers of the woods, the stoats and weasels with their much smaller snouts and their smaller frames and their far sharper predatory instincts.

When we got back I searched again, found in the wire at the corner of the aviary a little piece of bloodstained white down — now I knew where it had happened. And later I found her little red ring, lying just on the other side of the wire in that place, but hidden behind a flowerpot. No sign of her leg, which was no doubt carried off and eaten, as she has in her time eaten dozens of chick or mice legs. A carnivore can have no sympathy and no remorse; it treats living flesh just as a meal, and so Hesper would treat any small creature which was her prey, she too would tear and dismember it — it's no different, I understand that, but it doesn't make it any easier.

Nothing terrible had ever happened to her to frighten her before — she had never met with anything other than kindness — she was happy and fearless and scared of nothing, living her own sweet little life — then suddenly the smooth surface erupted and a terrifying monster leaped out and seized her, avid to rip her flesh, to drink her blood.

We brought her back from the vet's the next day. Though I had spoken to the vet on the phone, I did not believe she would survive the shock until we actually got there and saw her on that Sunday morning. He brought the box in and, without taking her out, took off the lid and set the box on the floor. We began discussing the injury, and then suddenly this little white heart-shaped face looked up, two bright black button eyes, and she gave that gorgeous little burble of recognition, very faint but unmistakeable — ill as she was, she knew it was us and was glad.

It was the last time we heard that pretty little note. Once she was home she retreated back into the twilight world of massive shock and trauma. She was totally silent, except now and then she would utter the most piteous sob-like cry, plaintive, weak and unbearably sad, so plangent and melancholy that it went like a knife to the heart. Her whole face had collapsed in on itself, so that she looked puffy and swollen, like a person with glandular trouble. Her eyes were swollen too, and appeared only briefly through lids which were always half shut. Her head was sunk down as low as it would go. At the same time she was extremely jumpy, and any sudden noise made her start in terror.

In the wild she would certainly have died, for she was incapable of getting food for herself and now we had to cut up everything for her because she was not able to tear it up by herself any more. I wondered sometimes about that pitiful sobbing cry, whether it was a recognisable sound to a barn owl mate, and would invite the compassionate act of feeding, of tearing up slivers of food for the injured bird.

Today is the first time she has begun to look around her again, has even begun to preen a little, though she still spends most of the time asleep, eyes shut. We are keeping her in the kitchen, in the old parrot cage — once or twice she has battered against the bars as if trying to escape, but mostly she just sleeps. Today the plaintive note has gone from her voice, and she can manage her old conversational gambits, but only weakly and at intervals — it is best not to rouse her too much.

18th August

Dismal day with Hesper, who though physically much recovered from her ordeal has definitely suffered something of a personality change. She hardly speaks at all, perhaps the tiniest little burble of a hello when you first go to see her, but the conversational hiss is never heard nowadays. It is disconcerting to speak to her and get nothing back but silence, never that wondrous little self-opinionated hiss of response. That tiny little interrogative note she always used to make to herself when exploring or examining something new, that's gone too.

She went back in the aviary on a permanent basis on Thursday, after five days indoors. By the end of that time she was getting very impatient with being restricted, and was liable to do herself more damage if we kept her in — she would try to get out of the parrot cage, spring onto the bars and hold on with her one foot, flapping and hopelessly struggling to run up with her phantom leg. Then she would stop and just hang there, her immensely long and narrow wings spread wide, making a beautiful white cruciform shape.

Now she cannot tear up her food by herself, a source of very great frustration. Neither can she scratch any itch, and sometimes in vain bends her head over and ruffles up her feathers as she used to do when she scratched her head with one claw, evidently feeling the need, yet failing to satisfy it and not understanding why. Her physical confidence has taken a severe knock — she feels insecure, vulnerable and unsteady — I can see that in every move that she makes. She teeters and shakes if I so much as touch her lightly with the very tip of my little finger.

When she has to move, it is with a horrid fat dead plop,

not the bustling self-important tilt-and-run of before. She still flies perfectly, but her landing is an inelegant crashing process, which seems to send a severe shock through her system. She is dented in confidence, humiliated and crestfallen. She doesn't even want any company. This morning when Jon went to see her and spoke to her, she was completely silent, did not turn round or react in any way — this is unprecedented, because he has always been a big favourite with her.

She spends most of her time asleep or just standing there motionless, looking rather grim and morose. She gets into the corner behind the logs, and stays there hour after hour, dozing or just staring at the wall.

She can no longer use her tree, and I have fixed up a long high perch for her instead. When she is up there, she spends most of her time busily cleaning herself up, erasing bit by bit the dried blood from her body and under her wing, gradually restoring the snowy purity of her underfeathers. She nibbles and nibbles and nibbles away at the caked mess.

She looks stupendously pretty, with the black gauzy teardrops on her white flanks, her little heart-shaped face with its special buff accentuation marks, her golden star- and cloud-flecked back. The puffed feathers of her breast are so superfine, so velvet soft, that they are far closer to the finest fur than feather. The quill structure of a normal bird's feather is present but it is so delicate it is impossible to feel it. If I touch her on her breast, my finger sinks an inch deep in the heavenly softness.

Because she is still weakly and very unsure of herself, she lets her wings droop down to aid her balance, and you see the lovely white underside of them, with their sprinkling of black teardrops.

It's not just me who thinks she's beautiful. Jon amazed by her. Brenda crying out rapturously 'Isn't she gorgeous! Oh isn't she gorgeous.'

I feel very sad that she will never be able to come to the glove again. She was doing so well at the end, flying eight or ten feet, negotiating the most awkward angles, and how enchanting she looked when she came gliding up and pounced with that little hissing roar of triumph.

Chapter Five - Hubert

19th August
The unfortunate little tawny owl, who has been overshadowed by all this drama, arrived the Monday after Hesper's accident, brought here by the son of the breeder. He was ten weeks old when he arrived, and I've had him for nearly two weeks now.

He has been named Hubert, after the fourteenth century knight in the French film *Les Visiteurs*. Pronounced in either the French or the English way, the somewhat clottish name suits him perfectly.

Hubert has not one particle of Hesper's grace — he's chunky and solid, strongly built, and very brisk and staccato in his movements. He's also extremely highly strung, scared by everything — a leaf rattling on the paving stones, a little bird dashing past — the dogs and cats send him into spasms of horror. When I slightly rocked the aviary tree whilst trying to adjust its position, he exploded off it and flew up into the topmost corner of the wire as if the tree was about to crunch him in its brittle green-stained arms.

In fact the slightest thing that changes in his immediate surroundings throws Hubert into forty fits. He was reared by hand, alone with his sister, from an egg. His reactions to change are so extreme that I imagine some science fiction scenario, the two of them kept in isolation from all other living beings, reared in a sterile white-tiled laboratory with a bright light burning twenty-four hours a day, their food being served by remote control, and nothing ever, ever changing in that shining white, hygienic, hermetically sealed tomb.

Fortunately, Hubert's behaviour towards me is not exactly in line with this stainless steel fantasy. He trusted me from the word go, spoke to me with his high rather piping chirp, and is affectionate and friendly in a rather anxious sort of way. He definitely doesn't like being touched, though, and if I persist he flies off, all brisk, abrupt and explosive, like a little brown bomb going off.

When he sees something that he hates (which is just about everything) he gives the most odd little clicking noise, which sounds exactly like someone popping bubble wrap.

He has still got a lot of baby feathers, dull and sheenless like burnt scrambled egg, but his wings and tail are those of an adult bird. These grown-up feathers are in nothing like as good condition as Hesper's even after all her sufferings — the tail feathers in particular are scrunched up, tatty, unkempt and disreputable. The main reason for this is he never grooms himself. I haven't once seen him preening — she does it all the time — she's cleaner and more fastidious than a little cat.

The texture of his feathers is very different from hers — they are not soft and silken, buoyant and puffery as if scarcely translated from air, but harsh, stiff, short, and unyielding to the touch. He's a nice little bird, though, compact, with surprisingly thickly covered legs and toes, encased in gold-beige felt like an eagle owl's. His eyes are immense — in fact they are freakishly so, huge liquid balls of black with an opaque bluish sheen in the centre. They have the most comical lids — a neat line runs all round them, coloured a very startling and striking raspberry pink — he looks like he's suffering from the mother and father of all hangovers.

Tawnies are supposed to be true nocturnal, claiming the very dead and centre of the night — barn owl are crepuscular, three hours on either side of dawn and dusk. Barn owls often hunt in the day when food is short or the weather has been bad — tawny owls hide out, concealed almost perfectly by their browns and blacks, the only thing moving their greyish eyelids which slide down slowly as they blink.

Blinking is a major deal with tawny owls. Hubert's eyelids are partially nude; the skin is bare on the side nearest the beak. This bare patch is a pale greyish-white which makes his blinking extremely emphatic, especially as at the same time he often used the third eyelid, the nictitating membrane, likewise a very startling greyish-white. All this makes him look like he has triangular eyelids and he spends hours perfecting his louche geometric blink.

Tawnies are known to kill barn owls in the wild, take over their nest sites. There is little other aggression, for their hours of activity don't coincide and the birds seldom meet when sharing a territory. It is easy to see how a tawny can kill a barn owl, because Hubert must be two or three times as strong as Hesper, and he is a male — the females are larger and can be very aggressive. They are well-known for attacks on humans when defending a nest site, often going for the face or eyes. On one or two well-documented occasions they have actually caused the loss of an eye — Eric Hosking, of course, is the best known casualty.

The experts in my books say that tawny owls are more active in an aviary, barn owls are the skulkers. 'They' also say tawnies are more fun, but my experience has been completely the opposite — Hubert hardly ever does anything at all. He spends all his time sitting right at the back of the aviary on Hesper's old tree — he never uses the available space like she does, the logs, the rocks, the floor, the water. There he sits skulking in the shadows, a real odd looking little fellow, with a fat head with no neck on a fat little body — he looks like an overstuffed teddy bear. Occasionally he sort of elongates himself — it is very bizarre — when he is puzzled, in a frisson of curiosity, he sort of gets longer and thinner all over, including his head, which one would think was anatomically impossible. So very long and thin does he get that he ends up like an upside-down exclamation mark.

Amazingly he only weighs 13¾ ounces, i.e. only three ounces more than Hesper before she began her training. You would think it was much more. He is definitely stronger than she is. When he takes off from the glove it is a real explosive force, a real kickback. His wings are short and powerful, not long, elegant and fine-bladed like hers, and this gives the tawnies their superb manoeuvrability in woodland and city, for they have conquered environments the barn owl cannot adapt to. Consequently their numbers are on the increase, whilst the barn owls inexorably decline.

Tawnies certainly have the air of being very tough little operators when you compare them to the barn owls' graceful evanescent charm.

20th August

There is a daft story about a pet tawny owl called Ruth in *Kilvert's Diary*, February 1870:

> [Miss Child] and her sister stranded in London at night went to London Bridge hotel (having missed the last train) with little money and no luggage except the owl in a basket. The owl hooted all night in spite of their putting it up the chimney, before the looking glass, under the bedclothes, and in a circle of lighted candles which they hoped it would mistake for the sun. The owl went on hooting, upset the basket, got out and flew about the room. The chambermaid almost frightened to death dared not come inside the door. Miss Child asked the waiter to get some mice for 'Ruth' but none could be got.

21st August
The first time that Hesper's been out on her log for days. She looks better this morning, an animated air, brisk movements, bright eyes, curiosity, turning to see a strange sound or sight instead of completely ignoring it as she has done recently. There is still no hiss, no conversation, but I've been bitten twice, hard, in the last ten minutes for impertinence — the discipline of the beak has been restored.

It's good to see, because for several days she was sunk in the deepest depression. In the worst part she spent all her time in a little crook behind the logs, or if she was on the high perch would face into the aviary, never out at the world as she always has done before. She was silent, never spoke, never reacted to coaxing. Nor did she ever investigate anything — her amazing inquisitiveness had totally vanished. She did not use her beak to test things or to respond to being touched.

The only hopeful sign about this twilight state was that she was still eating, not a lot, about half as much as before, but nevertheless enough to keep alive and well.

One continuing problem is that she is having trouble with mutes building up in her hinder parts, the white paste drying there and matting her formerly immaculate feathers. Normally the barn owls shit by sort of crouching down, lifting their tails and shooting backwards at the same time, to clear the waste right away from their bodies. She can't manage this any more, and consequently she is becoming soiled. I thought for a while it was because she could no longer physically reach these parts to clean herself, but in fact these birds are so wonderfully neatly built, so adroit and double-jointed, that she actually cleans between her legs by turning her face to the rear, reaching over her back, lifting her tail and nibbling as required, a contortion which she achieves with the uttermost airy effortlessness. It is not, therefore, the capability which has failed but the will to do so, and perhaps the sheer volume of the mess which has built up. Since she's got depressed, she is no longer so fastidious, doesn't groom constantly and has even left the old shadow of the bloodstains on the inside of her wing, a ghost of a mark on the gorgeous white.

We put Hubert's aylmeri on the other day. Doing this kind of thing has never been a problem with Hesper, but I knew Hubert was going to throw a very considerable wobbly. Jon insisted on trying our method with Hesper, i.e. just holding the bird gently, and for his pains he got the equivalent of an owl grenade going off in his hands. After that I did the trick Alan showed me and threw a towel over Hubert from behind. I held this muffled bundle, from which there issued a constant stream of absolutely furious imprecations and curses, while Jon fixed the aylmeri and got punctured badly — Hubert's little pale feet were lashing out whenever he could wriggle them free and once he drew blood. He never ceased fighting and struggling until at last I turned him rightways up and let him gently drop out on the log. He came out all ruffled and fighting mad, and was in a vile mood for the next 24 hours.

On the other hand, being highly motivated by food — it is his 101 per cent obsession and best pleasure in life — he has proved very easy to teach about coming for his morsels and then being cast off back onto his perch. Hubert is constantly ravenous and starving hungry no matter how much he gets, and the first two or three pieces he practically gollops your fingers down as well, so that you have to retrieve them from the back of his throat.

He's a bit of a prima donna all round. Temperamental, wilful and cussed. If he's in a nice mood, though, he is rather sweet — he cranes over the branch towards you, his little pale furry claws, which are very pretty, bunched together like little hands. He is by no means a beauty, but his looks are improving as he loses those dull frizzy baby feathers — they are real feathers, not Hesper's old amorphous fluff, and they collect in drifts in the four corners of the aviary. The first glossy brown dapples and scallops are appearing on his breast, growing behind the dull sheenless baby plumage, and looking as polished and bright as chestnuts in contrast.

27th August
Hesper was so full of brightness and curiosity this morning that I dared to do what it had seemed I would never be able to do again and very gently slid my hand under her belly and lifted her up on the glove. She seemed really pleased to be up there again, her most amiable voice. When I moved she spread her wings to compensate for the slight unsteadiness she felt but showed no inclination to escape. I decided to try taking her into the house, threading the leash straight through the ring of her remaining anklet. We went up the garden oh so slowly, having to stop every two or three steps for her to regain her balance. Though it looked highly uncomfortable, she did not appear to be unhappy about it. Only once did she try to fly off and she returned immediately to the glove. Her gorgeous wings were draped down over my arm. Her trust in me was very touching.

She was indoors in the kitchen for an hour. Not much happened but it was obvious that her old curiosity had come back, a delight to see.

28th August
Hubert and the footgame. Stroking his lovely little toes,

which have the softness of velvet, clad as they are in that very pale fawny beige with delectable little liver-brown freckles. I tickle him under the bare pads and he gently flexes his digits, tries with an easy placid gentleness to take hold of your finger, sometimes succeeds, holds it tight, but without digging his claws in.

He loves being tickled under the chin. Hesper has a manic passion for this and rolls up her eyes and closes them in ecstasy. They both have the sweetest gentlest manners, and use their beaks to caress you in their turn — reciprocal favours, so very polite.

Everything in Hubert's training has been easy, easy, easy — he has never minded about the jesses, the glove, anything — but the problem comes as soon as you take him outside the aviary, because he is totally and utterly paranoid of everything. He utters his explosive click whenever the dogs or cats hove into sight, or draws himself up, that elongated look he gets, and blinks very slowly but very frequently.

When he really gets himself into a state, he makes a flutter in his throat, the gular flutter, a sort of panting motion, just as I saw in Alan's more nervous birds.

The other day he saw Hesper as we walked through her aviary and went completely batty, bating off the glove in a volley of bubblewrap clicks, wings exploding. Hesper looked startled and bemused by all the commotion as I bundled the clot into his bedroom.

To get to his aviary I have to carry him through Hesper's, an arrangement which has both drawbacks and advantages. I hide him away from her, carrying him on the far side of me, concealed by my body, but he usually makes some racket which gives the game away. When Hesper discovers something odd is going on, she always gives the same bemused twitter. Hubert is hustled past her, under wraps, like a chap going into court under a coat escorted by zealous police officers.

Strange little note — he always craps in the same place. There is the odd exception, but as a general rule it holds true — his mutes almost always land in one spot and form a large wet squishy bull's-eye. It is probably because he seldom varies his position, almost always perching in exactly the same place. Even in her crippled state Hesper is infinitely more active than him. There are always little dots of white all over the place where she has been exploring and nosing about her chamber, but Hubert sticks to his one religious boghole.

His pellets are different from Hesper's, larger, much softer and very yellow in colour. If I don't pick them up quickly they disintegrate of their own accord and become indistinguishable from the sand. Hers are small, hard, black and compact, and hang about for ages until I remove them. She produces at least one a day. I think his are more infrequent, perhaps one every two or three days, though the fact they rot so quickly makes it difficult to be certain.

2nd September

Hesper sneezing, moisture running from the nares, excitement over food. New.

I was getting so concerned about the white paste matting her feathers that I decided I must help her with it. One morning, three or four days ago, as she stood high above me on the perch, I started rolling the paste between my fingers. It was a great mass of soft chalk — bits came off, then parts of the superfine feathers themselves, as if the build up of the waste matter had rotted them through. Hesper put up with this overfamiliarity quite patiently, though there were one or two outbursts of slightly aggrieved twittering. I was pleased with my handiwork, though she still looked a mess. Went away. Though I didn't see her at it, evidently she finished the job herself, because when I next looked she was beautifully clean.

I thought it would all build up again as before, but her leg is so much stronger now and she suddenly seems to have got the hang of what to do — fly down to the sand, do that funny little courtesy/dipping squat, and let fly. Her feathers remain spotless now.

As a pleasant by-product to this, she appears to have completely stopped crapping on my clothes. Or perhaps it is just that she is getting older and has better control of her bowels.

She's managing her disability much better, and has learnt several new ways to cope with it, for example a fairly stunning way of flying what is virtually sideways along the perch. She evidently prefers this stunt to the alternative, a laborious, undignified and annoyingly slow hopping. The pole is dead straight, and as nearly as is physically possible she flies sideways from one side to the other, without turning to face where she is going, a most impressive trick.

The landing in the sand is very daring and adroit now, she takes quite an aggressive dive at it, almost a pounce. As for travelling along the floor, she is just beginning to develop a method of using her wings to give her lift-off, so she can cover the ground more quickly and more comfortably — she obviously hates the fat ungainly plop.

She is also to my great annoyance running up the wire at the front again, using her wings to help her, and though she hops rather than runs she does it all so quickly that she doesn't appear to have only one leg.

The aviaries will soon be double-wired properly to prevent any repetition of the terrible attack on Hesper. At the moment I am making do with sheets of badly cut wire-mesh tied on with string, which gives the place the air of a chic gypsy encampment.

6th September
On our way to Arundel Castle, we stopped at Huxleys Bird of Prey Centre. Stormy wet windy day, but it had stopped raining by then and we hoped they might fly the birds after all. The girl at the desk said they wouldn't get the birds out now as they had already been fed. She gave us a reduced entrance rate as an apology.

We were the only people there — the place was deserted. It was beautifully, indeed immaculately kept, with a good layout and many flowers and interesting shrubs. There were numerous aviaries, mostly diurnal raptors and owls, but there was also very audibly a kookaburra with its long-drawn out maniac laugh, the sort of sound effect which goes with a dense Dartmoor fog and a homicidal felon on the loose.

The flying birds were in little separate pens under cover, each tethered with its own space of sanded floor. There must have been ten or eleven of them, and amongst them were two tawnies and two barn owls. The barn owls were nothing like as pretty as Hesper, bigger and coarser in build, with long lugubrious faces, and extremely long white legs as bandy as a cowboy's. Their markings were patchy and unattractive too. The tawny owls on the other hand were very pretty and friendly. Not so the little kestrel further up, who made to strike me with her neat bright yellow feet, evidently disliking my overfamiliarity. And near to her was a merlin, such a thrill to see that tiny bird, the smallest of all the British falcons. A miniature hunter of the most exquisite delicacy, with the fine lines and taut grace of all creatures built for speed. Its feathers were the loveliest dark glossy brown, a subtle and rare colour made all the more striking by their highly polished sheen, almost as bright as a newly shelled chestnut's.

The merlin looked very sweet for all its ferocity (they take skylarks), and it is hardly surprising that they were considered the best bird for a lady in the heyday of falconry in the Middle Ages. The merlin was for a lady; the gyrfalcon was for a king; the kestrel was for a knave (or squire) — the correct birds for each rank of society are so described in the *Boke of St Albans*, written by Dame Juliana Bernes, Abbess of Sopwell Nunnery, in the fifteenth century. Strange how these things come around: I see a mention of this lady every so often in my falconry books (and her name always has a different spelling), but years ago, long before I knew anything of her or had any interest in birds of prey, I went with three friends to the ruins of Sopwell Nunnery. Presumably it had been dissolved by Henry VIII, and most of the stones had been pillaged for other buildings, because now nothing was left but a few broken-down walls in thick undergrowth, massively solid pieces of masonry which looked as if they could survive an atom bomb. The top surfaces were crumbling but bound together with ivy, and we climbed up high and looked around us. The area was the backside of St Albans, some very insalubrious council estates backing onto a piece of rubbish-strewn wasteland. We posed amongst the ruins and Pete took several arty photographs.

That stray fragment of memory is very bewitching and I think to myself, pleased, 'So that was Dame Juliana's old home'. It must have been a wonderful place to live in the days of its prosperity, in that low rich valley with the watermeadows, the Ver wandering through the pastureland, and the huge grey Abbey up on the hill on the skyline. A kind of paradise, particularly if one had hours and hours to devote to falconry, with the dark evenings and the wet days when one couldn't go out being spent writing a treatise on one's favourite pastime.

The merlin was so delightful I really wanted one, but it would be grossly impractical — they need wide open spaces and someone dedicated to fly them, not the damp enclosed boskage round this house and me struggling to find half an hour here and there of flying time.

In the outside aviaries, I was amazed to see tawny owls and barn owls mixed together by some promiscuously generous hand. My reading had taught me to expect that they were ancestral enemies and that the tawny owls would slaughter the barn owls on sight. Here five dozy old bachelors lived in peace together, ranged in a long row on a perch. Further down they had long-eared and short-eared owls with tawnies. The man at the desk said the different species would accept one another quite happily if they were raised together.

There were several pairs of barn owls on their own. Again they were much larger and stronger than Hesper. They had a force in them which is way beyond her — one pair, for example, kept flying aggressively up to the wire in front of us, banging into it very hard with both feet, and then wheeling and returning to their perch. They repeated this sequence over and over again with exactly the same pattern, timing and ferocity.

They evidently considered us some kind of threat, and the repetitive behaviour was rather disturbing, it had the cracked gleam of insanity, so we moved on. Their aviary was a mock-up of a barn, quite fun, with a cartwheel, an old hay waggon, wicker baskets, etcetera. As an environment it is both exciting and potentially dangerous. When I think of all the obsessive care I have taken to make sure there is nothing back at home which might injure, cut or catch my birds!

21st September

Last Sunday Hesper in the kitchen — the first time she has come for a mouse since the accident. I held it up, not really expecting anything, and suddenly she came down on the glove with the most delicate finesse and confidence, so aerial a sprite you could hardly feel her land — it was as if a spiderweb was alighting. She took evident pleasure in her own skill. There is a certain rather smug and happy expression in her which shows that she is pleased with what she has done, that she relishes her accuracy and power, her adroit judgement of difficult angles.

She carried on talking while she was swallowing the mouse, so her voice became very wheezy and squeaky.

Once she had swallowed the mouse, she flew up to the top of the cupboard, but was only satisfied with the perch for a minute or so. Soon she took off again and went wheeling around the dark painted ceiling, which is twelve to fourteen feet high. Flying round against the dark background, her white underfeathers showed up very strongly, but it was not a particularly graceful sight — barn owls do not raise their legs when they fly but let them trail, and Hesper's one leg was jiggling about with the strain and stress of cutting round in a tight space.

She went round twice and then flew back to the top of the cupboard. A moment later she repeated the performance, and then again a minute after that. As she came overhead there was a strong downdraught from her wings. She was not flying silently, but making quite a racket. Yet she certainly has the capability for silent flight, and it can be very unnerving at times, thinking that she is in one place and turning round to discover her somewhere else completely different. She can move with absolute noiselessness, and, when my back is turned, deceives me even though I am constantly listening out for her to make sure she is not getting herself into trouble.

At last she alighted on the side counter, where there is a mirror propped up against the wall. She looked in the mirror, and then just like a cat went round the back to see who was lurking there. I doubt she recognised her barn owl shape, just saw some vague entity moving in the glass.

Later she played another favourite game — killing the floor mat. Something about the curled-up corners excites her wrath, and she dives down on one corner, head first, and strikes it with her one foot. She slays it and then moves to the opposite corner and kills that too. The classic barn owl dive, taking a header straight at the prey, then the feet coming forward, outstretched, extended, conveying the force of the blow through eight lethal talons. Or four in Hesper's case.

I don't think that I would ever have plucked up the courage to let Hesper fly free, even if she had never had her accident. She is so special to me. She is so entirely and utterly at ease with me that our interactions are those of one species, not two, and clearly that species is barn owl, not human, since Hesper is the one managing the relationship, not me. There is no barrier between us, in her mind at least. I find her perfect acceptance of me, and everything I do, is so delightful that her company never palls.

I remember her when she was little, and still lived indoors, sleeping behind my feet as I wrote in my notebook. She had spent an hour exploring, rampaging about, and now she was tired. The place she crept to be warm and safe was in the cave made between my ankles and the sofa. She slept there happily in uttermost peace. That perfect confidence reposed in something as alien as a human. I think that is the thing about her I shall always remember best, that and the awful day we went to collect her at the vet's and this little heart-shaped face looked up at us from the cardboard box and uttered that gorgeous little burble of welcome.

28th September
Hesper doing brilliantly at the coming for supper bit. Difficult and tricky angles, ten or twelve feet, no problem. Her confidence has entirely come back, so once when she missed Jon's glove and tumbled down onto the floor, she was not in the least put out — a little twittering, but she came again at once without hesitation. Falls with her are not the serious matter that they are with us. She is so light that she can get in what looks like a truly dismal scrape and emerge from it without the slightest bit of damage, her twittering conveying the mildest annoyance with herself as if she is exclaiming 'Dear me, that was rather careless of me'.

She is different in one sense, though, since the accident. One very very rarely sees that hyperactive fidgetiness she used to have, never still, flapping and beating about. She is curious, lively, interested and as conversational as ever, but the frenetic fizz has gone off it. Mostly one sees her in a state of serenity, a profound philosophical peace which is rarely shaken.

I meant to make a note on the vexed question of crapping and having her in the house — the timetable appears to be roughly two minutes after she is first brought in, she will let fly, either on the spot where I have put her down or from the top of the kitchen cupboard onto the stove (easy to clear up if one is quick enough with the newspaper). The first crap is a big one and usually pretty wet. Subsequent numbers are very small, and seem to have something of the consistency of double cream though naturally they are nothing like so delectable or fragrant.

Neither sort is difficult to wash out, though in a perfect world one could happily do without them.

1st October
Been rereading Sheridan Le Fanu's *In A Glass Darkly*, one of

my favourite books. It must be a while since I last looked at these stories, because now, with my head full of Hesper, I notice for the first time that a barn owl stars in *The Familiar*, being a party to the final horrific madness and terrible death of Captain Barton. His fiancée has adopted the bird as a pet:

> Young ladies are much given to the cultivation of pets; and among those who shared the favour of Miss Montague was a fine old owl, which the gardener, who had caught him napping among the ivy of a ruined stable, had dutifully presented to that young lady.

It is clearly a barn owl, because the story refers to 'the well-known sound, more like a long-drawn gasp than a hiss, with which these birds from their secret haunts affright the quiet of the night'. The bird thoroughly unnerves and upsets Captain Barton, who has already been made very ill by the figure of a man who constantly haunts him. Finally the denouement is reached: a bloodcurdling yell breaks the night's silence; the rescuers rush in too late to save the Captain; and the owl makes its exit from the death-chamber in the most spectacular way:

> Without waiting for inquiry or explanation, Montague, closely followed by the servant, hurried to the chamber door, turned the handle, and pushed it open. As the door yielded to his pressure, the ill-omened bird of which the servant had been in search, uttering its spectral warning, started suddenly from the far side of the bed, and, flying through the doorway close over their heads, and extinguishing, in its passage, the candle which Montague carried, crashed through the skylight that overlooked the lobby and sailed away into the darkness of the outer space.

Wow! Grossly improbable, but wow. That's a real Hollywood scene for a bird.

9th October

Yesterday in the garden with Hubert. I had tethered him and placed the bow perch under the drooping hawthorn, now covered with hundred of little hard red fruits. Suddenly the tree was full of little flickering sprites, the long-tailed tits, but instead of their usual delightful musical fluting, they were all uttering one horrid abrupt gruff little tut. Flickering and twinkling through the leaves, there must have been at least eight or ten of them, all coming down through the branches in a mob to scold the owl.

The long-tailed tits are my very favourite birds after Hesper. They are very very tiny and extraordinarily pretty — charcoal-black, pearl-mushroom, faded-rose, silver-white. They travel in small family groups, flickering lightly and usually invisibly through the trees, and all the time constantly singing to one another, the most delightful ethereal fairy-like music, as silvery and haunting as tiny elfin bells. It seems to me they must have been at least part of the inspiration for the legends of the fairies, in their flitting, their only partially glimpsed movements, their slight forms and muted old-velvet colours, and their delicate otherworldly song.

Then there also came down two blue tits and an exquisite tiny goldcrest, all chiding and scolding the owl. Something of the commotion must have attracted a jay, which zapped past and also screamed abuse at him. It was a strange moment, as if I had momentarily acquired a cloak of invisibility — all had eyes only for Hubert and ignored me sitting only seven feet away from them. Hubert paid very little attention to them, staring round at everything else apart from them. After a while he decided to try to hoot, a somewhat cracked and inaccurate impression which came out sounding extremely funny.

He looks very much more handsome now his adult feathers have come through, splashed markings of white and black down his beautiful brown breast. His feathers have a lovely gloss to them; they are like heavy brown silk to the touch.

Another improvement to his appearance — his eyes are far more in proportion to the rest of him now, not so wildly freakish in appearance. I don't know that they have actually changed size or shape, but what has certainly changed is the startling raspberry-pink rims they used to have which made him look so disgustingly hung-over. The colour has now faded so much it is hardly noticeable and his looks are consequently greatly improved.

Hubert keeps being very audibly mugged each night by the neighbouring wild owls, who fly down, sit around in the nearby trees and shriek abuse at him. One of them lets out the most bloodcurdling shriek apparently right outside my window every night at three o'clock in the morning.

20th October

Humming and hawing about what to do with Hubert, who grows wilder and more difficult every day. I think a lot of that is my fault. I had decided I really must commence training him in earnest, but I only managed two intensive days before work took over again.

During those two days, I made several errors, none of which did anything to improve the situation. I was fitting him with jesses, swivel and leash afresh every day, unlike Alan and most falconers who put on all the kit and leave it on — their birds are permanently tethered. I wasn't even leaving the jesses on Hubert in the aviary, because not having them in all the time worked so well with Hesper and indeed is imperative now she has only one leg. Hubert difficult about having his legs fiddled with, and I would get the jesses through the ring holes almost by stealth whilst he sat on the branch of the tree above me, threading them through, then attaching the swivel, then threading the leash through the swivel, all the while he regarding me bemused, evidently wondering what I was up to. Then would come the time to take him up. One morning he bated at exactly the wrong moment and ended up all hooked up, hanging upside down, and of course absolutely incandescent with fury. This and similar faux-pas have increased a hundredfold his dislike of being handled. Another time, I had him on the bow perch in the yard and lightly sprinkled him with the hosepipe, one of those treats Hesper used to adore (she has not had such a treat since the night before her accident — I never have her out on the bow perch now). A little light shower would, I considered, improve Hubert's appearance and be good for his health — he is still a major scruff-bag who never tidies himself up. He reacted very badly to the water, started floundering madly about, fell into the puddle that was collecting, and got an even greater dousing, his wings saturated, draggling their tips against the ground. I cut off the water, and he hopped back on the bow perch to dry out with the most harassed and demented expression. He sat there stolidly for an hour in the warm autumn sunshine, never spreading his wings out to dry as Hesper used to, never once preening himself, and looking more like a bird who had disgustingly had black treacle dumped all over him than a bird who had simply got wet.

The soaking did him good, though, because later, when he was thoroughly dried out, he looked very handsome, trim and in fine fettle. His breast feathers have little filmy lacy fanlets over the more structured black, cream and fawn splashes, and the effect is very attractive, a sort of misting and softening of the otherwise very bold markings.

There is no doubt that Hubert is hard work. I have probably been utterly spoiled by Hesper, who has always been such a friendly and agreeable little soul, frightened of nothing, and always full of inquisitive curiosity. Hubert loathes anything new, and explodes off in a frenzy when I try to touch him, because he resents the trapping of his feet, the restriction of the jesses. Hesper never made all this song and dance about it. Since she lost her leg, I have not used jesses but had her on the leash alone, threading it through the ring of her anklet and tying it with a double knot. The first time I carried her she tried to fly off once, but she has not done it since — she seems bright enough to understand the difference between the two situations, which Hubert certainly doesn't — for example, the minute we get back in the aviary he tries to take off for the inevitable bloody tree, never waiting for me to get the tackle off and consequently giving himself yet another severe shock when he is brought up short.

He needs many many hours spent on him, and I just haven't got them. I have been thinking of finding another home for him. I discussed it with Alan, and may swap Hubert for one of Alan's adult barn owls. But when I said this to Jon, he said with mild indignation 'You can't get rid of Hubert!' Then he asked with a laugh, 'Don't you like him?' I felt like Hubert was the poor fat boy at the back of the class whom everyone picked on and that I ought to be lending moral support to him. 'No, he's much less fun that Hesper and consequently I don't spend enough time with him.' But now I began to feel deeply guilty about Hubert, and I decided there must be some other solution.

I finally decided to move him out of the big aviary into the small one, which Buddy used to have. It is much more open, having wire down to the ground on two sides. He has two branches at different heights, a log, a bath, and the nestbox which is entered by a large square aperture (but he never uses it). He has to get involved whether he wants to or not, and apparently he does quite like it. There has been an immediate improvement in his connecting with life now he can no longer skulk in the shadows at the back (though if skulking were required by him he could go and do it in the nestbox). He sits looking out at the sky and has grown to tolerate the near proximity of the dogs and the cats — he's given up clicking bubblewrap at them, and just watches them now, a little slyly, his grey eyelids sliding triangularly over his eyes. The nicest thing of all is that he has become much more one of the family, you can get up close to him whenever you want to without having to go through the paraphernalia of unlocking doors — he is in bright light, and it is that which has shown me quite how pretty he has become — he has all of a sudden grown exceptionally sweet-looking.

After the brief distraction of the move, Hubert has got back to an even more frantic obsession with food. We have an outburst of hysterics at every meal. It can be somewhat disconcerting having this owlian Molotov Cocktail going off in your face each time you visit him, and so I have taken to opening the little door into the side of the nestbox and leaning in and calling 'Shop!' and the next instant this brown bustling frenetic dashing little bear crashes in with a godalmighty thump and runs up and grabs the food as if he hasn't eaten for a year and runs out with it again.

He has also, wonder of wonders, started taking baths. He never went near the bath in his old aviary, either to drink or to bathe. I sometimes saw Hesper drinking, taking those little revolted fastidious sips of hers, but Hubert never. When I moved him, I thought 'Why bother to give him a bowl?' as the weather was no longer very hot. But after a couple of days I relented and gave him his old bath back. The same night he obviously went into it, for the next morning all the water was gone, bar a sluggish sandy half-inch in the bottom, and Hubert was sporting half-dried tail feathers.

All in all the move has been a success.

Hesper meanwhile is in very peevish and crotchety mood. I think it may be something to do with the fact she is getting more feathers through — they stick up here and there, still in their protective coating, sharp narrow greyish scrolls which have inevitably led to her being called 'Spiky'. I remember she was in this peevish mood when she was getting her adult feathers, she hated to be touched, and would bite hard if you persisted. It must be fiendishly itchy or sensitive. This afternoon I wanted to check a mark on her face, to see if she had scabbed herself or it was just some leftover meal. She got absolutely fighting mad when I held her, the first time she has been so furious; she started hissing in a very very aggressive, angry and emphatic way, a warning sound which rose up into a crescendo of maniac fury. It was momentarily quite daunting. Then as I held her, scolded her, tickled her face, suddenly she fell silent and stopped struggling.

The weather is still very mild. I loiter about in the yard as it gets dark, feeding the owls, and then after I have locked up I still hang about with the dogs, peering through the wire — I can never have enough of the owls' beauty. Two or three nights in a row now Hesper (whom I feed first) has given the same piercing screech as I emerge from Hubert's aviary — it is the equivalent of his hoot, and thrilling to hear, the first time I have ever heard a barn owl screech. It is very challenging, hostile, stark and eerie, far more eerie than the tawnies' commonly heard Twit-Twoo.

Chapter Six - Albina

22nd October

I have just brought back from Sussex near Horsham a new baby barn owl. She is the eldest of the third brood of the year, the owls breeding so prolifically because of the prolonged warmth of the weather. She is five weeks old, the same age as Hesper when she came here. Why have I got her? So that I will have a barn owl to fly free, because I hope she will be company for Hesper, and as a coward's insurance policy because Hesper would leave such a colossal gap in my life if she died.

I thought long and hard about getting a mate for Hesper. The breeder knowing her birds very well, and having hand-raised over a hundred baby owls, could guess their sex fairly accurately from early colouration as the adult feathers began to inch through. She considered she had two females and a male, and I could have the choice of any of them.

I did not make a final decision until we were down in Sussex and I could discuss it with Sue. Sue was straightforward and no nonsense. When I voiced concern that Hesper wouldn't manage with only one leg, she said 'Oh they'll manage fine. He'll just get her in the nest box and do his business there.' She said that even confirmed imprints would mate. An imprint is a bird which thinks it is a human (or perhaps that humans are birds and that real birds are something else altogether). Unable to see the difference between itself and its keeper, it is liable to project its romantic impulses on a biologically unsuitable mate. However, Sue thinks that barn owls can overcome this false conditioning (which is contrary to what I understood from my books and Alan) because barn owls 'are like rabbits and do it just for fun'. She added that they were at it all the time and, once you got a pair, you would be knee-deep in baby owls before you could blink.

This year her hen had twelve eggs in the first clutch, and nine in the last — I forget the number of the middle one, but it was similarly large. From this last brood Sue has only kept five of the eggs and removed the rest. She is hand-rearing three, one died in the nest of unknown causes, and one she has left with the mother, 'I always like them to have one baby to rear'. She said if you wanted to stop the hen from continually laying and incubating, you could buy a clutch of little fake eggs and put them in the nestbox.

I decided it was best not to get a mate for Hesper, not yet at any rate. But I wanted to know if she and the other female owl would get along, would they enjoy one another's company, would they be friends? Sue was very confident that this would be so. (Again this is contrary to what Alan said, which was that they needed to be introduced at a young age or they would never accept one another.) I was convinced by her certainty, and having decided they would be friends, now went on to the next stage of worrying which was, having become bosom pals, would one of them pine if at some stage in the future I got the other a mate. Sue said 'No, not as long as they can see one another.' 'Or all three could stay in the same aviary' suggested Jon. 'No, absolutely not, one of the hens would try to kill the other' — they would fight so ferociously that murder would be committed.

We talked for a while about the projects for releasing barn owls back into the wild. She had assisted in one in Sussex, on an immense farm, the woman owner of which had pots of money and did up a barn at the centre of the farm 'just for the owls'. They had been there for four years now, breeding very happily, and were now feeding themselves, no longer needing to have their diet supplemented.

Sue said to me, 'Have you ever seen a wild barn owl's nest?'

'No.'

'They're absolutely disgusting. It's a wonder that any of the babies ever survive, sitting in filth and it's crawling with maggots...'

We went out to have a look at the parent birds, a very brief look so as not to disturb them. They have a completely open aviary, just wire on all sides, but a shed attached to it, with a door and holes for the barn owls to enter by, and inside a very snug nesting box on legs, perhaps five feet off the ground, with a flap at the front which can be let down for observation. The father was standing on top of the box, drawn up on one leg, looking very solemn, prosperous and Edwardian, practically smoking a cigar. She was inside, the little one cuddled up next to her. They are tender parents, he feeds her and she feeds the baby, tearing off tiny slivers of meat for it until it is old enough to feed itself.

I was a little anxious when I saw the parents as they were very much the type of barn owl we saw at Huxleys, the ones I wasn't over-keen on. They are study and strong, and in some ways rather crude-looking, far less fine and delicate than Hesper's family strain. Indeed the new baby is a thumpingly solid little thing, and probably weighs over a pound. She has a great fat turkey body with a tiny head on top and much sweaty fuzzy white baby fluff. Her beak is a hatchet beak, and definitely bigger than Hesper's even at this stage (though, come to think of it, I seem to remember reading that the barn owl youngsters achieve their final size in a matter of 6-7 weeks and after that it is the complex business of growing the feathers which takes all their energy).

As for looks, there is the characteristic absolutely vile witch's hideousness. She hold her claws out in front of her as she sits exactly like a witch's fingers, the long elongated digits with talon-like nails.

She is rather jumpy and twitchy. She is startled by sudden noises and not laid back like Hesper. Her nervousness affected her stomach and she had diarrhoea on and off for the first six days. She is a little frightened of me, and utters a warning threat whenever I approach, though mostly the bars of the parrot cage prevent her from seeing the true horror of my appearance. Yet by rights she should be even more adaptable, for in the first three weeks of her life she was taken everywhere by Sue, even in the car, on the road, because Sue has a job as a sales rep. Perhaps she is missing her siblings, with which she seems to have a closer relationship than Hesper with her one brother/sister. When I saw them at Sue's house, they were all huddled together in a mass of surgical off-white, little angular witch faces pointing upwards, cute, and very snugly and sweatily warm together.

Her voice patterns are different. She does not have Hesper's delicious little burble, but only a funny little chittering with notes far more staccato and chopped up than Hesper's. I have heard no hiss as yet, except the deep vehement roaring hiss with which she greeted the appearance of the cats and dogs. She hates them. Again this is quite unlike Hesper.

I'm very interested to observe the differences between this new owlet and Hesper. Do barn owls have characters in any marked way? Could the differences which are already apparent between them be due to their quite obviously different genetic heritage?

29th October

The owlet has had about seventeen different names already, and it is getting tiresome. Her official name is going to be Albina, even though I am not entirely happy with it. Albie or Binnie (as in Binnie the Bastard) seem to be the favoured diminutives.

The introduction to one another went splendidly. First I brought Hesper in the kitchen with me for the afternoon while I did some work. She flew around a little bit and then settled down. Albina was in the sitting room, in her parrot cage, as I did not want to upset Hesper by letting her find someone on her territory when she first came in. The plan was to let Hesper have an hour or two with me in peace, before I brought the usurper to her notice.

About half past three, when Hesper was dozing on top of one of the kitchen cupboards, I slipped into the sitting room and got the parrot cage. I brought it in and set it on the counter. It was about fourteen feet away from Hesper, and some five feet lower down. As I sat down to watch what happened, Albie gave a little chittering cry.

Hesper's reaction was instantaneous, immediate, and extremely startling. The placid laid-back easy-going Hesper vaporised, to be replaced by an implacable avenging Fury. She went almost black with rage, every feather stiff with it, and drawing herself up to her full height of ten inches, she launched herself like a thunderbolt at the cage. She landed on the counter right next to it. The owlet looked out. There was appalled shock on both sides, the shock of recognition, and then both rushed headlong into battle. They were separated by the white plastic-coated bars of the cage, which are quite narrowly set together, so there was very little chance of them making actual contact. But still they clopped their beaks and dashed themselves at one another, almost apoplectic with fury. They slashed at each other with their beaks, and the hard beaks made the bars ring and clash, so that it sounded like two minuscule knights in armour. Had they not been separated there would have been the most massive punch-up.

At last they drew back from the first engagement.

Hesper was clearly livid. Her most characteristic sign of anger is a completely immobile stony silence and stillness. Now she stood there motionless, utterly soundless, and stared and stared and stared relentlessly, never blinking, never altering her position or her gaze one iota. She was a tiny owl Medusa, who would sizzle the life out of that lummock turkey with her death-dealing gaze.

The lummock turkey looks plain horrified by this antagonism, and, though by no means crazy about me, glances at me rather nervous and worried for an ally. I draw my chair up to the fight, willing to be umpire but I'm not going to intervene.

Albie having taken her eyes off her opponent for a few seconds now returns them in the same direction, and, seeing the horrid vision again, charges — very courageously for such a young thing, even though of course she is a third as much again as Hesper's size. Again they engage, beaks clopping and pinging against the wire. It is getting so heated I say 'Break it up, break it up!' and for a wonder they stop at the sound of my voice. They recommence staring. Hesper would win hands down at the staring contest. She is rigid, and so intense that the hatred practically beams from her eyes in rival-incinerating gamma rays. Her posture is forward, head sunk down between her shoulders in the most menacing fashion. She does not deviate from this stance one millimetre but keeps it held for five minutes at least. The baby, fazed by this manic stare of disapproval, acts very like a cat does when outfaced, and starts a little preening and brushing up, studiously pretending not to notice Hesper. Seeing her enemy's guard has slipped, Hesper's frozen posture melts for a nanosecond and she leans almost imperceptibly forward to get a closer look. Astonishment is what you see on her face now, absolute astonishment and amazement. Albie catches the movement and looks up, and Hesper turns to stone again. Ten minutes of impasse. I start writing these notes and Albie is distracted by the scratching and rattling of the pen and forgets Hesper and watches me instead. But Hesper does not forget and relent — instead the little gorgon carries on staring and staring. She narrows her eyes to slits to make the effect still more horrid. The youngster, reverting to baby ways — or just not capable of this intensity of loathing — now looks embarrassed and ill at ease, as if she has found herself in a social situation she wants to get out of but cannot think of any way of doing so. She pushes her gaucheries so far as to start scratching her head, loses her balance and almost falls over. Whenever she looks away, Hesper momentarily unfreezes and peers at her, only to transform immediately back to stone the instant Albie looks in her direction.

Albie gives up the unequal contest, and does a bit more cleaning and brushing up, and even hisses at me to remind me that the dinner hour is long past.

In the end, I gently whisk the cage away, shut the door on it, and return to Hesper. Hesper looks rather surprised that the enemy has vanished, but now it is All Clear she is perfectly relaxed and forgets all about it in thirty seconds flat.

I have to say her unmistakeably vicious reaction was a revelation. This is an owl who is so laid back she is practically prone, who has taken dogs, cats, and many strange things in her stride, who has lost a leg through her insatiably enquiring curiosity, and yet the instant, the split second that she heard Albina's little chitter, reacted in the most hostile and violent way possible. Weird. Very odd.

5th November

Third confrontation between Hesper and Albina (the second going no better than the first, though in the end Hesper got bored and, disengaging, flew up on the fridge). The dishwasher is on at the moment, and Hesper didn't catch Albina's little chitterings as quickly as before. She continued up on the top of the kitchen cupboard, in her favourite place, where she can crap all over the stove. Albina meanwhile had seen her at once, and was all agog, crouching down with fear and caution, but completely fascinated, fixing her bright black bead button eyes on her.

Wishing to stir things up a bit, I take Hesper down from the top of the cupboard and put her on the glove. I walk up to the cage. Hesper catches sight of Albina, clops her beak, but seems generally disinclined to bother with her. She has always been at her softest and most affectionate when on the glove, when you can caress her and she caresses you softly back. Hesper looks out of the window, where the cat is mewing persistently on the windowsill and causing an annoying diversion. Opening the door the minutest crack I let him in, and boot him out of the kitchen into the hall. I sit down on the chair.

And now Hesper decides to intimidate Albina. She flies over and lands six inches away, with the most surly, slit-eyed and threatening expression. She spreads her wings out in menace. The exquisite loveliness of her wings never fails to move me — how lovely they look now with their silver stars, iron-grey bands and subtle shades of gold. Spread wide, how exquisitely revealed is their precise geometry, each blade lying so crisply on the next, the long elegant primaries, the shorter secondaries which are so pleasingly patterned and so exactly and perfectly measured in size.

Hesper has abandoned the gorgon pose for today. Instead she acts as if she is taking part in some impossibly recondite and antique Japanese ritual, a piece of such elaborate ceremonial precision that it must have been refined over a thousand years at least. She bows her head, and very slowly shakes it from side to side, her wings arching out beside her with extreme grace and yet so stiff and mannered that they resemble sacred fans. Slowly, slowly she raises her head. Then slowly, slowly she lowers it back down, and once again she shakes it, slowly, slowly, slowly, epitomising her loathing, her disbelief, her rage. Her posture is hunchbacked, horrid, shoulders high, and head low, the eyes glaring between half-shut lids. She clops her beak. Her expression is one of the most intense malevolence. She repeats the ritual. Albie stares aghast.

Some minutes pass. Hesper refurls her wings and goes back to staring. All of a sudden something sparks them both off and there is a flurry of activity. Hesper's wings come out again. Albina just bounces up and down like a rubber ball to show she is just as keen to fight, just as willing. Hesper doesn't deign to approach the wire. She merely focuses those death-dealing eyes, a laser beam boring down on her pathetic rival. Albie, being a baby, blows her cool by waggling her head about and not keeping the correct glacial stillness and stiffness of demeanour. Hesper evidently considers she is a pisspoor rival, ignoring the fact she herself is only half Albie's size and moreover only has one leg.

As before, I remove the cage by a sleight of hand, and Hesper looks momentarily surprised and then just accepts it.

A frosty moonlit night. Last night at five o'clock there was a mist before the almost full moon. Hesper is always especially lively at this time, and the moonlight doubles her crazy edge — she flies white and mothlike round the darkling aviary, searching for a way out, and then comes up to the wire and hangs on it, her great white wings a cruciform shape in the blackness. Her mood in these crepuscular hours is so different from the gentle somnolence of day. I guess I never really saw this side of her before, because it would take place so much later in the summer, when I was indoors in the house, whereas now that the clocks have gone back I am seeing it every night. She and Hubert are like an orchestra tuning up, flying up against the wire and then back into the shadows. They're spooked, rattled, superactive, longing to get out in the moonlit garden, dreaming dreams of the hunt. It is at this time that I wish I could set them free. But Hesper would be dead within hours and Hubert would starve, so it would be an insane thing to do.

You hear the wild tawny owls out early too. They have not come close to the garden for quite a while, they seem to have given up harassing Hubert quite so terribly. Perhaps they have realised he is a captive and presents no threat to them. Or perhaps they have simply discovered that they can't physically get at him. Were they to find him flying loose, they would probably mince him. It is much too easy to forget that the wild world is divided up into the most jealously guarded territories, fenced off by invisible demarcation lines policed as ferociously as Checkpoint Charlie. The local tawnies 'own' this garden and its environs, and have already made their feelings about Hubert quite clear.

13th November

I startled a heron on the pond in the woods this morning, coming up the bottom path with the dogs so quietly that it did not hear us until we were right at the pond's edge. Our sudden materialisation obviously gave it a severe fright, because as it climbed up into the narrow circle of sky above the pond it let out a long white string of waste matter. The bird was slate-grey, very thin; it looked like a youngster. The moment it raised itself above the canopy of tall trees round the pond, it was set upon by eight or ten crows, some of which I realised had been lurking in the trees just for this moment. It flew off, in that slow ungainly way herons have, towards the railway, closely pursued by the flapping black hoodlums who didn't seem particularly animated by spite but more by a sort of have-a-go mentality. Either they had nothing better to do with their morning, and were hanging like yobs round the corvine equivalent of a bus shelter, or else they thought they might harry the heron into disgorging its pitiful meal. It can't have got much to eat from the pond, which is so sunken in level since the vandals broke the dam down that there can only be the odd tiddler or frog to catch. The heron looked the very embodiment of famine, with its hatchet head, storm-grey flanks, and trailing long skeletonal legs.

The closest I got to a heron was startling another one, fishing in the stream, several months ago. Because of the high banks, it didn't see me and neither did I see it until we were right on top of one another. Suddenly a great gaunt shape rose up and ascended in circles into the sky. There was something almost prehistoric about its shape — it looked like one of those early flying reptiles, the link between the dinosaurs and the birds. It was incredibly emaciated and angular, with its spear-like beak, its skeletal form, curved neck and trailing stick-thin legs. It was coloured a particularly sombre, even sinister grey. Its flight was very slow, gawky and inelegant; it looked as if it could hardly raise itself up on those great, grey, ragged, bony wings.

The sky was thunderous, a dark iron-grey; the bird was grey-steel against the black thunderclouds. Incredible to think they used to hunt these birds with falcons, chase them for miles and miles on horseback — it even had a name, heron-coursing. That is what the picture at Gleneagles was about, the one of the heron sicking up its breakfast.

When the herons were pursued, they would disgorge their food and ring up (climb in circles) to keep above the falcons. Working as a pair the falcons would try to seize the heron's neck and bind onto it. The combined weight of the falcons would force the heron back to the ground and the falconers who galloped up afterwards could reclaim their birds and kill the heron — or sometimes merely ring it as a trophy and set it free if they were not of a bloodthirsty disposition. However, if gyrfalcons were used on the herons, these powerful birds might stoop (dive in attack) so hard that they could kill or cripple their prey.

Sometimes tame herons were used as decoys, or else in a rather disgusting modified form of the sport. They were force-fed, and then their necks were bound to stop them from jettisoning their food, the supposition being that the extra weight of a full crop would slow the herons down and make it easier for the falcons to tackle them. After the chase the tame herons would be allowed to disgorge, and all the food would come flooding out — frogs, snakes, fishes and co — as in the picture at the hotel.

Hubert's had a change of personality all of a sudden. I went away for two days and he was a completely different bird when I came back. Barbara, who was looking after the establishment, told me over the phone she was a bit worried about him because he wasn't eating. When I came back on the Sunday, he looked fine, bright eyes, perfect feathers, his usual fidgetiness, in fact there were no signs of sickness or ailments of any sort but he had suddenly — just like that — lost his mania for food. He is eating one third of what he used to before, and probably not before time either because the last time I weighed him he was over a pound. But I wouldn't take the chance of cutting him down in the cold weather, and now he is doing it for himself. If it didn't seem such an odd time of year for it, you would almost think he was in love. He has come over all cuddly and friendly, and for the first time since the contretemps over the jesses will allow me to touch him, will nibble me affectionately with his beak. I though he might like to recommence the old foot games, and he was agreeable, but they are too downright painful for me now, as he is no longer gentle with his talons but curves them round my finger and slowly but inexorably tightens his grip, an effect which is like being pierced by tiny red-hot knives.

Other than that, he is affectionate and companionable, talking all the time in a soft whoo-whoo voice. But all his former really appalling neurotic nervousness has come back. It is almost as if the leaves falling off the trees have really freaked him out, the sudden opening out of our woodland space, the sheer brightness of the light that pours into it now. He spends his time looking wild-eyed into the new depths of the sky, starting and jumping at every new sight and sound.

If I walk past his aviary with Hesper and just to tease him bring her up close to the wire, he puffs himself up to the most immense size, swinging his head madly up and down, to and fro, in order to get his bearings on her. He looks like a gigantic puffball mushroom, almost perfectly spherical, a ball splashed all over with soft sable, silver beige, and chocolate markings.

Because Albina will soon get to the stage when she can no longer be kept indoors, I'm putting her out in the aviary for a few hours every day. She doesn't like it much. Like Hubert, everything alarms her. When my shadow, cast by the autumnal sunshine, walked up the wall behind her, she almost had a fit.

It is very noticeable that she is far more possessive over food than Hesper ever was. I guess this must be the result of having to compete with two siblings. If I give her something and she doesn't manage to bolt it all down at once, she goes crazy if she thinks I am moving in on it, and, snatching it, runs away into a corner, mantling furiously over her treasure.

The weekend that I was away she dropped what seemed like three-quarters of her baby fluff in a mere two days. Barbara had to hoover up, because great snow clouds of the stuff were billowing everywhere. The fluff is extremely fine, and gets in your throat, where it is very difficult to dislodge. Now she just wears a frill of dense fluff round her lower body, as if sporting a ballerina's tutu or a rara skirt. It is a comical effect but very sweet.

Thankfully, despite my misgivings, she is now promising to be a good-looking owl. She is bigger and stronger than Hesper, and her colouring is far less delicate, but she has her own distinctive charm. Her eyes have a liver-brown sheen in some lights, and the accentuation marks on her face are also tinged with liver brown as opposed to Hesper's beige gold. She has a much more heavily spotted breast — there are plentiful spots on the undersides of her wings and even spots on her coffee ruff.

19th November

Bitterly cold weather for several days. I've been very concerned about Hesper with her one leg — she cannot alternate feet, warm one up in her undergarments whilst the other grips the cold wood of the perch. The annoying little thing won't go in her box, which is sheltered and floored with newspapers and an old T-shirt. Her foot is almost bare, with only a very light dusting of white delicate hairs which must be too slight and thin to keep her warm. I am wondering if I should have some heating for her, but the aviary is not designed to conserve heat — it has too large an open-wired front. Perhaps, however, I am worrying about nothing.

This morning I very gently laid my fingers over her toes to test how cold they were, and they appeared to be perfectly warm — they were not glacial and stone-dead as our fingers would be after gripping a length of freezing cold wood all night. Hesper in her nice gentle surprised mood, blinking eyes, looking curious — 'What are you up to?' She seemed fine, and showing more of those little rolled grey spikes where new feathers are coming through. I decided the best thing to do is just feed her as much as she can eat and redesign the box layout to make it more enticing.

I have been praying for damp weather and comparative warmth, as crisis time for Albina is approaching just as it did with Hesper in June. It's been easier to keep Albina quiet and pacified in the parrot cage, because she has never been indulged so much, let out so much, made such a fuss of, and has therefore accepted the confined space more easily. However, her days in the aviary have given her a new independence, she's learnt to fly just like that, and all of a sudden she's getting feisty and impatient, and when brought in at night bangs against the wires of the cage trying to escape.

Because it has been so freezing cold, I have tried to acclimatise her by keeping her in the study at night, the coldest room in the house, with the window open a little way. Still not as deathly cold as outside, though. The situation tense and getting tenser — can I get her well enough adapted to the outside while the temperature difference remains so extreme?

I go out to the aviary to see her, and she hisses away madly. I feed her, and she eats like a horse as usual. She flies down onto the sandy floor at one stage and starts to shiver, drawing one foot up into her soft feathers but trembling with cold. I feel the sandy floor — it is icy-cold, morgue-like, radiating the most deathly chill. 'Silly little idiot, stand on the box.' I put her on the box, a comparatively warm surface, and she stops shivering.

With Albina's new-found ability to fly has come a sudden amazing increase in confidence. I've had her loose in the kitchen with me in the last two days, and from being rather nervous, starting back if I approach her, pecking and biting when touched, she's suddenly all over me, trampling on me with her cold sticky little feet, running up my trousers and getting on my shoulder as if we've always been the most amazing bosom pals. I'm amazed by the change in her. Only a week ago, she couldn't tolerate being touched in any way. I made a deliberate plan of spending ten minutes every day handling her, getting her out of the cage, placing my fingers lightly on her feet, touching her beak with the tip of a finger, placing a hand gently on her back — all of these attentions she treated with every appearance of appalled horror, starting back until the wall stopped her, then, unable to get any further, drawing herself upright to avoid these loathsome caresses as much as possible, all the time uttering a warning hiss and attempting to bite. When she bites hard, it can be quite painful. I tapped her beak in reprimand once or twice for the severest nips, though I was very unsure of whether this was a sensible policy and thought on the whole it probably wasn't and so stopped it. But that's academic now — suddenly she can't get enough of stomping all over me and trying to get bits of food out of me, convinced I've got them secreted all around my person. She is crazy for food, she eats well over twice as much as Hesper, who has never shown this maniac obsession with the stuff. Like Hubert before he put himself on his self-imposed diet, Albina is constantly ravenous, constantly starving, and her stomach is a seemingly bottomless pit.

She has got very amusing and endearing all of a sudden — before I felt rather cool and uncommitted about her, but she has become such fun, with her wayward hoydenish manner as she stomps about in what feels like Dr Marten boots, that I can see she is going to be competing with Hesper in the favouritism stakes soon. She has suddenly got so ballsy and full of herself that she attacked the cat tonight. Bunny was sitting peaceably in her little box under the counter when the owl flew down to the floor about three feet away. She turned round, saw the cat, and hissing madly and arching her wings in threat literally charged the cat with such a determined pugnacious I'm-going-to-sort-you-out-you-fluffy-fuck expression that Bunny quailed in horror and shrank back. I whipped Albina away before she could make contact — 'Now that really isn't a good idea'. Thirty seconds later she flew down deliberately to the same spot and charged the cat again. The scene came back to me when I was in bed and had turned out the light, and suddenly I couldn't stop laughing.

20th November

A gang of jackdaws seem to have moved into next door's oak trees, and it is very cheerful and pleasant to wake up to their lovely chucking call.

The morning is lit by a lovely soft hazy opalescent light. Huge flocks of crows in the fields, cawing and flapping about lazily. The fields behind us have turned completely to slime where the farmer sprayed the entire acreage with weedkiller. He never harvested the crop that he turned the kestrels off for. But then leaving the crops to rot on the ground happens three years out of four with him — he is a completely useless manager of the land. I suppose he is getting a subsidy for this pathetic pretence of keeping the farm viable. Every time I see the wrecked fields I'm infuriated — why not leave them fallow for the wild life to enjoy?

The afternoon is mild, with trailing clouds and soft colours. The mortuary chill has gone off the air today — I decide this must be the night when Albina takes her chances in the open air. She has been in the aviary all day, and I have fitted her out with a box and a rag to sleep on — all should be okay. Instead of bringing her in before dark, I leave her out there. Later, when I take the dogs out before bedtime, it seems much chillier. The clouds have cleared away, the stars twinkle like little bits of ice. Shall I or shan't I bring her in again? I know there may not be another good chance if the cold weather sets in in earnest. I harden my heart and go to bed. Just as on Hesper's first night out, I spend a sleepless night. In the morning there has been a frost, a light dusting over the grass. I rush out expecting to find a rigid corpse. Albina is perched on Hesper's old tree, tall, white and upright, like a Christmas fairy. She looks definitely chilly but bright, alert and well pleased with herself, even smug.

It is very noticeable now that Albina is next door to Hesper in the daylight how much darker and more heavily spotted she is. The line under her chin is tinted with black, her face is pure white, the hood a deeper gold, the coffee ruff wider, the spots not gauzy and delicate but quite distinct and sprinkled with a very lavish hand. Her colouring is not so subtle, and sometimes that makes her look garish, and at other times it has the reverse effect and makes my gorgeous little Hesper look drab.

Albina and Hesper could live twenty years in captivity and if they did so they would probably be pure white. The markings and patterns, the golden buff with iron-grey bars and stripes, melt away over successive moults. The wing tips and tail are the first to become pure white. The primary moult pattern, the sequence in which the owl sheds and replaces the critical flight feathers, one pair at a time down the length of the wing, and the tail feathers which govern balance and manoeuvrability, takes three years to complete. Barn owls are so dependent on silent flight that their moult takes much longer than other birds of prey who usually get it all over in a month or two. In a lifespan of twenty years, a bird would have five or six moults of the primaries, losing colour every time, becoming gradually paler and paler until at last it resembled the true churchyard ghost.

Albina's feathers have a different texture to Hesper's; they are less puffed and buoyant, more clotted and dense, almost cottonwoolish. They feel damper somehow, as if they have greater absorbency of moisture and are taking some of the winter chills and wet out of the air. Perhaps this is why she appears to feel the cold more, because otherwise she is far more solidly built and sturdy and yet it is only her you ever see shivering.

She has a different smell from Hesper, stronger, more obviously owly, probably because of the different texture of these feathers. Her domestic habits in any case are far more slapdash and slatternly — she craps in her box — Hesper never does.

Another habit Albina has which is not so delightful is, being a greedy little vulture, she snatches voraciously at her titbits and then shakes them about violently, so that if there is any blood or ichor on the thing it splatters everywhere and especially over me.

She is an amusing little creature, though, very irritable and prickly about her amour propre, greeting any liberties taken with the greatest of severity, a chiding scolding tirade and some pretty painful nips of the beak. She must have learnt early on that these nips make people draw back their interfering fingers very sharply, because whenever I with colossal stoicism ignore her and carry on touching her she looks a little mystified and slightly peeved that her usual methods aren't working.

If I continue to ignore her biting for long enough, she will gradually calm down, even with a suffering air allowing me to stroke her soft breast. A few more minutes of soothing and she actually begins to enjoy it a tiny bit, closing her eyes, and standing on one leg. But she is at once startled back into action by any sudden movement, and as soon as that happens she starts biting again. She doesn't inflict serious damage, doesn't break the skin, but it is a nasty pinch. Better if I turn the back of my hand towards her, because then she can't get any grip.

12th December

Writing with Hesper in the kitchen with me.

At first she was very sleepy and tired, and just sat on the kitchen table next to me, blinking heavily, occasionally snoozing, but always answering back in a woozy sleepy voice if I spoke to her. About an hour after coming in, she brought up a pellet, a very small one, and immediately took on a more wakeful and alert air, turning her head rapidly, looking around all sharp-witted and bright-eyed. Whereas a human will tend to turn their head and focus on one thing, or else pan slowly across a vista, in this mood when she is almost electrically charged with energy, Hesper's mode of looking around consists of a series of tiny snapshots, a number of 'takes', each from a slightly different point of view. Once she knows the lie of the land perfectly, she launches herself off into space. As soon as she has alighted, being Hesper she immediately speaks to herself in a little musical twitter — 'That was okay, what's next?' — a constant subdued conversation with herself that I have not heard from either of my other owls.

It has been nearly a month since I kept these notes up. The usual thing — too much going on in the world of boring old human affairs. Now all I have left to guide my memory is little scribbled hieroglyphics on the backs of crumpled bits of paper.

At the end of November, I first flew Albina on the creance. It was one of those mornings when suddenly I felt only impatience and contempt at my previous cowardice about flying one of my own birds, and quite on the spur of the moment decided to try it. It went like a dream. Albina took very little notice of the garden after the first five minutes, all her attention being focused on me and the fascinating bribes of chick she was getting. I flew her at least twenty feet, on the big lawn — an enormous thrill getting her to come to me.

The following day I tried again and it was so simple and easy with her that the day after that I set her down on the grass completely free for the first time. It took her all of 30 seconds to make the first jump to the glove. I kept the session very short, perhaps ten minutes at the most, keeping away from the trees and the bushes, in the middle of the grass. Once I walked to the foot of the stairs down from the kitchen, and set her on the tall flowerpots there, meaning to walk away and call her to me, but I had hardly gone six steps before she was after me and landing on my shoulder, still keeping up her continual hectoring for food. After that she went down on the grass, and I had her back to me once more and secured her jesses, stopping the session before her attention ever had a chance to wander.

The next day I showed off our achievements to Jon. With the two of us there we could call her over greater distances, from one to the other, and take great pleasure in watching her fly, that lovely sequence when having dipped down she swoops up again to land in a flutter of white on the glove.

It is a truly amazing feeling. And yet oddly enough this thing I've looked forward to so much for so many months was in a sense an anticlimax. In the end it was not difficult — it was overcoming my own extreme nervousness which was the hard thing. Now I have done it I am almost cagier than ever about it. Such excursions will never have the relaxed air that taking a dog for a walk does, but will always be an occasion for vigilance and extreme caution. Truly I have a great deal more fun with the owls in the aviary, where I am not in such a constant state of paranoia about them. My ideal would be to have a large barn to fly them in complete security — howsoever, the chances of this ever happening are remote in the extreme.

Excursions for Albina were in any case put a stop to suddenly by the change in the weather. The autumn was so mild and balmy that the leaves did not all come off the trees until the end of November. We went from autumn to winter virtually overnight, a cold blast from Siberia bringing what felt like Arctic conditions after the soft mushiness of the preceding weeks. Snow began falling on 5th December. The first day it just turned to slush as it fell — big flakes, sticky and adhesive, spinning down flat as plates out of a wintery sky. They fell more and more thickly in the afternoon, so that the rate of melting did not quite keep up and a wet thin covering remained on the bushes. I went out to feed the owls at four o'clock, wearing my usual waterproof jacket with the hood up, and caused them all a severe attack of nerves, appearing so strangely covered in white blotches. They realised very quickly that it was me when they heard my voice — as soon as I spoke they answered me, Hubert with his soft whoo-whoo, Albina with her loud imperative hiss, and Hesper with her slight musical twitter which one has to be close to hear. But I recognised all the more strongly how much their identification of me is based upon what I am wearing, the distinctive markings of my apparent plumage — any dramatic change in my clothes brings a little crisis, and it was a while before they were blasé about me wearing the hood of my jacket up. Jon, who visits them sporadically and almost always in something different, they do not greet with any rapture any more. Hubert took particular exception to his white trousers. Nor does it mend matters when Jon speaks to them. Hesper certainly should remember his voice, but she has become very distant with him, and very tetchy when he tries to stroke her — a positive glare of fury sometimes, very much as if she would like to strike him dead. She has not forgotten him altogether, but she is markedly cool now towards her former favourite. She does not see him often enough for her to remember him well, and she shows little tolerance towards his intermittent visits.

After the snow fell, it thawed overnight and the next day was similar weather, snowflakes falling thickly, melting as they came down but not quite quickly enough to keep up. A light covering remained, tenuous, thin, irregular and wet-looking. For a day or so it looked as if we were going to escape the worst effects. Then the temperature began to plummet, it grew appallingly cold.

I was in a constant state of anxiety about the owls. This is the first winter that I have gone through with them, and I had no idea of what to expect. I was particularly concerned for Hesper with her lone leg, no ability to tuck the foot up in the downy undergarments.

All of them became exceedingly grumpy and sullen as the chill deepened. Once, in a previous spell of cold weather which had only lasted a day or so, I had gone to check Hesper's foot, found it was warm when laid my finger gently over it. Now that it was so bitter cold I tried to do the same thing. Went out early the first morning to be greeted with a very frowsy and ill-tempered looking bird. I tried to check her foot and she got unutterably furious with me, biting savagely and uttering little squeaking red-hot cries of rage. I thought it would be easier to check her foot if I held her as I have done before, with one hand holding her still against my body, but she only got even more maddened, absolutely livid with fury, her cries full of maniacal threats, so that I decided it would be best just to leave her to it and went away.

I wonder how she sees me, truly thinks of me — as a sister, as an irritating mate, as a parent that just won't go away?

I have no idea.

I decided to get the owls through the freezing weather by stuffing them all to the gills with as much as they could eat.

By the second day of the big chill Hesper had slightly brightened up, was bright and breezy and brisking about in the aviary when I went out to see her. The snow had melted and refrozen, and a solid layer of ice covered the paving stones. When the dogs walked across it, their feet made cracking noises at every step. Hubert banged about his flight in a paranoid flap when he saw the pair of them crunching across the snowy background.

Albina was the one who suffered the most. She would have little shivering fits, her foot up in her feathers, her body all fluffed up, and an expression of acute misery and discomfort on her face. The cold seemed to disorientate her, for when I called her for food she overshot the glove twice one morning, a thing never known before.

I was also suffering, my fingers chilled to solid ice each time I had to open and close the padlocks on the doors. The locks kept freezing and it would take an age to get the warm key into them, and then slowly wriggle it about until it imparted enough heat to release the mechanism.

It was a peculiar sort of snow, very gritty and adhesive. Once it got on your clothes you could not shake off because it just remained there as if glued. This was a particular nuisance if I brushed against any laden tree or bush, which immediately dumped its load down my neck or into my wellington boots — it was just not possible to shake the damned stuff out so it would all melt and make me even colder.

There was very little snow lying on the trees or bushes. Walking in the fields in the mornings, I saw the hawthorns so thickly covered with their small hard red fruits that from a distance, set against the snow, the trees appeared to be oozing blood, like the enchanted trees in Dante's forest.

Despite such largesse, many birds were obviously starving. There were four herons at the pond before it froze over, sharing the very lean pickings to be had there. The huge flocks of crows disappeared suddenly, virtually overnight — now all we have left is a few scattered individuals. I wonder if the crows have just moved on, or if many of them were casualties of the freeze.

Albina was eating six mice a day at the height of the cold weather. Hubert, still on his self-imposed diet, caused me a great deal of anxiety by picking at his food in the most distrait and anorexic way.

15th December

The snow has been gone for nearly a week now and so I shall get back to training Albina.

She is certainly a character — she is full of bossy and amusing familiarities. Hesper is evanescent, gentle, wraith-like — Albina is the complete reverse, stomping about in hobnail boots, making her box reverberate like a drum, and hissing so loudly that you can hear her on the other side of the garden. However, she has a vein of noticeable timidity. Hesper's confidence in me is unshakeable. Albina's clearly is not. If I go into the aviary and start cleaning it out, making unfamiliar movements, striking odd postures, Albina retreats into her box and looks out at me nervously, all of a sudden just like a little baby again.

For the most part, however, she is pretty full of herself. When I go into Hesper, talk to her, feed her, I can hear the constant loud hissing of Albina through the interconnecting door. If I don't attend to her immediately, she begins to batter the door with impatience. There are horrible scratching and ominous banging noises, as if the next door chamber is haunted. When I open the door she often tumbles in, sometimes from a height of three or four feet or more, as if she had walked vertically up the woodwork before it opened. I have to be quick and grab her, otherwise she shoots in, scuttling over the floor. If I whip her out quick enough Hesper doesn't even see her, and so peace is preserved — Hesper looking round, hissing to me 'What's going on?', misses the form of her hated rival.

They are no closer to making friends. I used to take one outside and stand in front of the other's aviary, showing off the loathsome form and hoping that by repeated exposure they would get used to one another. In fact their enmity only seems to deepen. Hubert is more laid back about them than they are about each other. Hesper went beserk the last time I tried this familiarisation routine, uttering the most raucous scream of hatred and hurling herself so violently at the wire that I thought she would do herself a serious injury. The one time she caught sight of Albina in her aviary she made a tremendously loud and aggressive hiss. It looks like they will always have to be kept apart, because Hesper is of an unforgiving nature, and definitely will countenance no rival. Albina, I feel sure, would be friends if Hesper would abate her murderous hostility a little bit, but there is not the slightest glimmer of any relenting on Hesper's part.

I guess she must see her aviary as a nest site, one which has to be rigorously defended. Unless misfortune strikes, barn owls in the wild don't move far from the nesting site which they chose in the first year of their lives — they remain faithful to the place and map out their territory around it. They are consistent in their movements, following chosen routes along roadsides, ditches, hedges, and streams. Many barn owl sites are traditional, and have been used by generation after generation for centuries. Yet barn owls are considered not to be particularly territorial as a general rule — they don't carry on like tawny owls, guarding their patch as ferociously as medieval warlords. Sometimes pairs of barn owls even have overlapping hunting ranges, and share the fringes equably so long as the immediate area of the nest site is not impinged upon. Tawnies are by no means so benign.

At night as soon as I open the backdoor the owls begin to call to me. Hesper's dainty little voice is lost at this distance, becoming obvious only when I turn the corner of the house, but the other two can be clearly heard. Albina hisses with great vigour, especially if she is feeling hungry, a very common state of affairs with her. But it is Hubert who is the star performer at night, completely making up for his somewhat samey performance during the day. He has a variety of voices — the soft whoo-whoo, a shrieking hysterical seesaw cry, and the traditional tawny call. Best of all he makes the most peculiar lunatic giggle; it sort of bubbles in his throat with a mad glee, like rain gurgling in the gutters and drainpipes of Bedlam.

If I go to see the owls, they all peer out at me, talking constantly, which has a most endearing and winsome effect. I take the torch down there with me, a very powerful beam which can spotlight the topmost branches of the tallest trees on the embankment, but I keep it pointing at the ground as I approach the aviaries. The little circle of moving golden light fascinates them and they follow it with rapt attention. The first time it appeared, naturally it frightened them. Equally predictable was the rate at which they got used to it — Hesper became blasé about it almost straightaway; after a while Albina also grew used to it; but Hubert continues to suffer it in his usual suffering neurotic way — he has never truly learned to accept it.

Hubert at night and the concert of the owls. The neighbouring tawnies call, and call, and mock and insult him, and he energetically returns the compliment. The garden sounds suitably haunted and ill-omened:

> The night has been unruly; where we lay
> Our chimneys were blown down; and as they say
> Lamentings heard i' the air; strange screams of death,
> And prophesying with accents terrible
> Of dire combustion and confus'd events
> New-hatch'd to the woeful time. The obscure bird
> Clamour'd the live-long night; some say the earth
> Was feverous and did shake.

The obscure bird now seems to be slightly calming down, abandoning the acute state of mania induced by the autumn leaves falling off. Yesterday he very gently accepted a gift from me, for the first time for six weeks, and tentatively, almost thoughtfully, carried it to the end of the branch to eat it. He looked utterly delightful as he walked along the tightrope branch, one foot after the other, balancing perfectly, in a very slinky and comical way. Branches are evidently very much a natural element for him. I have never seen him on the ground — the barn owls are down there all the time — but he makes up for his lack of terrestrial confidence by being tremendously adroit and neat in his movements along the suspended network of branches.

Hubert began to eat and very daintily picked out the entrails from the chick he had so politely and gently accepted from me. His manners were immaculate. I did not stay long to stare at him, in case it annoyed him, but in fact he never seems to regard me as a potential thief — he does not mantle over his meal as Albina does.

If he does not finish his meal, he stashes the leftover bits behind the cardboard box in the nesting box. I wondered why the cardboard box kept getting moved about, and then one evening when he didn't feel like eating straight away he took the chick from me, exploded off in his brisk way into the nesting box, and gave the cardboard box a hard impatient shove to get it out of the way. He put the chick between the box and the wall. Again there was no appearance of him attempting to hide it from me. It is supposedly the sign of a true imprint that it regards a human being as a rival for its food.

Christmas Eve

It is Christmas Eve, there are lots of things to do, and it is late afternoon and nearly twilight before I go to take Albina for her walk around the garden.

Tonight she is not in her usual hyped-up mania for food, but looks around her with intent curiosity. She is both mesmerised and rattled by the pools of shadow in the bushes, the crepuscular spaces, the rustling sounds of the trees, a last walker going home whose footsteps we can hear behind the fence, the single rusty street light filtering through the bare branches. It has got very chilly, and the sounds echo on these bare cold evenings, so much so that a train going up the mainline seems to be in the siding across the lane. A red railway signal twinkles up on the embankment, a strangely evocative and friendly gleam. It always makes me think of nineteenth century Russia, intellectuals stranded in the dull blankness of the provinces, for whom the train line, over hundreds of miles to Moscow, represented the route to civilisation, and thus was an inconceivably romantic thing.

In the fresh evening air I can smell Albina's characteristic scent. She has been living outside for some weeks, perching on her tree, no longer festering in her smelly nest, and has taken several baths, but there is no mistaking the fact that Albina has a graveyard perfume. When she opens her mouth you can smell her bad breath, a rank concentration of carnivorous pong. Hesper is almost as cuddly as a teddy bear in comparison, with the same dry warm comforting nothingness of scent. I still think this must have something to do with the different nature of their feathers, the peculiarly spongy and absorbent quality of Albina's, although the main drawback in this argument is that it does nothing to explain Albina's appalling halitosis. Perhaps she is just genetically programmed to stink.

Hesper's feathers are, as usual, utterly immaculate. Now that she has grown a thicker down to cope with the cold weather, she looks untidier than before, softer, plumper, and more dimpled, like the most celestially luxurious feather pillow, but still she is the most neatly made and pretty little creature. Albina is more handsome, but her looks are flashy and disreputable. Her tail feathers are all broken and bent, and like Hubert you never see her preening.

I take Albina back in before it is too dark to see. Back in the aviary she gets very irritable about me trying to take the jesses out of her anklets and gives me a few tetchy nips. A sort of tussle develops. She is getting flappy and histrionic, but when I speak to praise her 'Good girl, good girl,' she stops instantly and looks back at me — intently, observingly. I've seen her do this before, suddenly fall quiet after being in one of her biting pecking states — it is impossible not to believe that some cognitive process is taking place, some dim recognition of the benign nature of my intentions towards to her which counteracts her natural instinct to make difficulties, the usual enormous fuss about having her feet fiddled with. It is as if, to her great surprise, she has once again suddenly observed that there are rewards other than food to my company. If I have ever seen a bird think, I would say that it was at this moment when so suddenly Albina falls quiet and looks at me as if assessing me differently, with that slightly wondering and bemused eye.

In this moment of uncharacteristic stillness on her part, suddenly I manage to get the jesses off by some never-to-be-repeated sleight of hand.

Albina does not look intellectual for more than a moment. All higher thought processes are instantly jettisoned the instant her supper comes out. She grabs the dangling body of the chick with violent rapacity, and flies away with it down to the log in the corner where she usually eats her food. I walk up to leave her another piece as well and she suddenly claps right down over her meal, wings and tails spread wide, head bent down over it, protecting her booty from any fell intent. She looks almost like a vampire bat as she hangs over it, avid and full of the most jealous passion for it — there is almost something leathery and obscene about her posture. She thinks her prey is not safe enough, and now she grapples it in her beak and stumbles off to the other corner of the log away from me. That still isn't enough, and so she flies into her box, the paper floor of which soon comes to resemble a badly maintained abattoir.

I leave her to it and walk back through Hesper's chamber. Hesp is glancing over her shoulder and hissing loudly, to make sure she attracts my attention. How beautiful she looks. I remember so well the first day she was out after her accident and how I saw her from the yard, at a sideways angle, on her high perch. Her little head was drooping, bowed down with immense gracefulness. It was a very strange and uncanny vision, for she looked for a few moments exactly like an angel, the classic Victorian graveyard angel, with face bowed and wings raised slightly away from the body in a pensive, protective and most graceful stance. Her pure whiteness and the hood of gold on her head aided this strange but very beautiful illusion.

Her looks have great changeability. In one of my books it says that someone once called barn owls 'Monkey-faced owls', and it is very true — in some lights Hesper really does look like a little monkey — there is something melancholy, wistful and simian about the shape of the face and the large, black, intelligent, speaking eyes. It is only the rapaciousness of the beak which gives her away, and most of the time that is concealed by the endearing little white whiskers round the mouth, leaving only a pale ivory-rose hook which could almost pass for a nose.

I think of all the good times I've had with Hesper this year, how much fun she has been, and yet in a curious way what little impact she has made on my life, a hovering shadow passing on a bright summer day, the wisp of frost in winter which melts as the sun rises up. The human world is too vivid, too brightly lit, too garish, too loud, too full of raucous noise — there is all that constant banging, screaming, trivia and razzmatazz, and it blots out the magic of the twilight of the owls.

Speaking to Hesper, looking up at her as she peers down at

me, I have a brief delicious fantasy about becoming an anchorite, living on a mountain with only my owls and other birds for company. I would spend hours and hours doing nothing but gazing at them, making notes on them, sketching them, meditating on their beauty and their strangeness. A placid drifting dreamy kind of existence, and totally at odds with the Protestant work ethic. How long would I seriously be able to keep it up?

It is very nearly dark. As I go back to the house, it is obvious that I and the dogs and Albina wandering about in the garden have kept the little bluetit from his bed. He roosts in the porch every night. He comes up to the house around quarter past four, earlier if the afternoon is cloudy, flying across the grass in a looping dipping flight. If anyone is around, he can't get to his sanctuary.

Now I see him fly away again into the hawthorn to wait for me to clear the area. I call the dogs and go inside. The light is on in the kitchen and up he comes swooping again and sees me at the kitchen window — it's enough to scare him — once more he's off. Then I kill the light and stand away from the window in the shadows, and by and by he comes looping up again and lands on the string of the wind chimes, looking around with intent jerky movements. The cat suddenly jumps up onto the windowsill, and he gets a severe shock and vanishes. I bring the cat in, stand back in the shadows once more. The little bird is desperate to get inside before nightfall, and hardly a minute has gone by before he's back again. He lands on the wind chimes once more, looks around, flies into the porch, looks around, searching intently for some murderer spying on him, at last considers that the coast is clear, hops up into the roof beams and is gone. I don't see the exact spot he vanishes. Once he is inside, as on every night, he will ignore all the comings and goings, the bright porch light being switched on, the ceremonial clapping of hands to frighten off the foxes otherwise Sasha disappears for hours chasing them, the letting out and calling in of the dogs. Safe in his little cubbyhole, he will sleep till dawn, emerge and vanish before anyone else in the household is awake.

There is a rather charming old superstition about Christmas Eve. On this one night alone in all the year, between twelve, the hour that Christ was born, and one o'clock in the morning, the animals and birds are said to have the gift of human speech.

If some bygone farmer had gone into his byre at midnight, he would have been able to understand exactly what was being said by the horses, the oxen, the sheep, the fowls, the cats, the mice, and the barn owl on the roof beam, and naturally they would all understand one another and be holding a sarcastic conversation about him.

I have decided to test this superstition out in a spirit of strict scientific enquiry. Experiment naturally requires staying up way past normal bedtime, watching rubbish on television, and drinking excessive amounts of whisky as a means of staying awake.

I tell Jon of my plan. Entering fully into the spirit of things he enquires 'Is that twelve o'clock Greenwich Meantime or European Time?'

No point in answering except to remind him that we are talking about imaginative leaps of faith here, something he does not know very much about. Jon laughs in that particularly nasty manner he has when he can't keep up with me in the idiocy stakes.

Just before midnight I go outside with the dogs. Jon remains indoors in the warm. The night is very mild — the clouds have come in and the chill has gone off the air. The red light still winks up on the railway embankment, in amongst the immense black pines. Above the trees arches the orange Home Counties sky, dull, claustrophobic, the colour of trash marmalade.

Midnight comes. I have confidently assumed that the bells in the little church up the valley will now ring out a peal of gladness. Instead each and every church in the vicinity is silent, and as a substitute we get fireworks, people here and there on the fringes of the estate letting off sundry bangers and rockets. Sasha has a severe phobia about fireworks and forthwith jumps right out of her skin, so that now there are three dogs in the garden, one normal, one naked and one merely a furry envelope.

Now Jon comes out to join us, fag in one hand, glass of beer in the other. I walk up to the aviary and demand of each of the owls in turn that they speak to me in human language. The owls adore midnight visitors, they are always extremely talkative and interested when we unexpectedly turn up at this hideous hour. Hesper and Albina hiss with great friendliness and enthusiasm, while Hubert makes his soft whoo-whoo.

I go up to Hesper's wire. I can see her little face peering forward, the little grey spikes, her new feathers, sticking up all around it. Hesper's eyes are bright and full of amusement.

I say to Hesper as a tease, 'Why don't you speak English?'

And she hisses back madly, 'Why don't you speak barn owl?'

Appendix

The survival rate for inexperienced barn owl youngsters is 25% in their first year.

Barn owls are extremely lightly built and conditions for them in modern Britain are most unfavourable. A census in 1932 estimated the number of breeding pairs in England and Wales at 12,000. In 1987 in Britain and Ireland as a whole, the population was estimated at 5,000 (a decline of 69% over 50 years). In some areas, there are no longer any barn owls at all. Others have been very badly affected — in Cornwall, for example, which should be a good wildlife habitat, latest estimates show that there are now only three barn owls in the wild for every ten a decade ago.

5,000 barn owls a year are killed by cars alone — that represents 52% of annual barn owl deaths. Barn owls are extremely vulnerable to traffic, because they fly low and comparatively slowly. They are not only hit by cars, they are threatened by them even when hunting on the verges, for they are so light, so floating and thistledown light, that they can be sucked in by the slipstream of one vehicle and killed by the next. It has been estimated that they can no longer safely nest within three miles of any motorway, dual carriageway or major road. This rules out vast swathes of country. There are only decreasing patches of habitat in a hostile landscape threaded through by mile after mile of road.

Barn owls have also declined in numbers due to changes in agriculture. Their golden heyday was around the turn of the eighteenth century. Early nineteenth naturalists describe them as being fairly common. The meadows and pastures were not overgrazed as they are nowadays, and so shrews and voles had natural cover, could build the little scuttling runs they use to colonise fields, and could therefore breed and be successful. Inefficient methods of harvesting and storing the grain, the loose rickyards and grainstacks of every farmyard, and the constant necessity for fodder and bedding for the horses, kept the white owls well supplied with mice and rats.

Nowadays there is little wastage of grain, so rats and mice have dropped in numbers, and rodenticides have cut them still further. Shrews, voles and field mice have been hit also. 95% of hay meadows have vanished since 1945. Instead farmers grow temporary meadows of single species of rye grass, which are cut frequently and don't allow the vole and shrew population to build up. Tree cover for these essential elements of the barn owl diet has also gone. An estimated 140,000 miles of hedgerow disappeared between 1946 and 1974. Woodland was being lost at a colossal rate even before the Second World War. Though woodland is not a natural barn owl habitat, the fringes of it have always been eminently suitable. We've lost 35-50% of our mature woodland since 1933.

All these statistics have been heard so many times that they have almost lost their power to shock. As far as the barn owl is concerned, it is an unremittingly dismal picture — except for a few isolated areas, the species is under the most intense pressure in the wild. That is why you cannot release tame or even rescued wild barn owls back into the wild without a DOE license. There are very few places where such released birds will survive.

Estimates of barn owls living in captivity in this country vary, but they certainly run into many thousands. Barn owls adapt very well to living with man because of their gentle and accommodating nature. They breed easily in captivity, and the long-term future of the white owl is assured. It is extremely sad, however, that few of us will ever have the joy of seeing these extremely beautiful and haunting birds as wild creatures flying free.

Bibliography

I am indebted to the following books for information:

The Barn Owl, by Colin Shawyer, published by Hamlyn, 1994

The Barn Owl, Mike Read and Jake Allsop, published by Blandford, 1994

The Complete Owl, Michael Leach, published by Chatto and Windus, 1992

Owls, by John Sparks & Tony Soper, published by David and Charles, revised edition 1989

Eric Hosking's Owls, by Eric Hosking with Dr Jim Flegg, published by Mermaid, originally published 1982 by Pelham Books, Mermaid fourth impression 1995

Owls of Europe, by Heimo Mikkola, published by T & A D Poyser, 1983

Birds of Prey of the British Isles, by Brian P Martin, published by David and Charles, 1992

Training Birds of Prey, by Jemima Parry-Jones, published by David and Charles, 1994

The Art of Falconry, by the Hon Gerald Lascelles, originally printed 1892, modern edition by C W Daniel Company Ltd